THE HARD TRUTH

THE HARD TRUTH

Simple Ways to Become a Better Climber

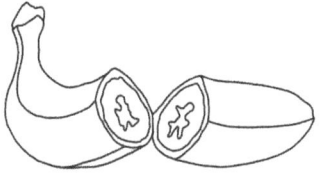

Written by Kris Hampton
Illustrated by Brendan Leonard

Copyright ©2020 by Power Company Climbing

All rights reserved. No part of this book may be reproduced or utilized in any form, or by electronic, mechanical, or other means, without the prior written permission of the author.

Written by Kris Hampton
Illustrations by Brendan Leonard www.semi-rad.com
Cover Art and Author/Illustrator Portraits by Kris Hampton
Edited and Designed by Brittany Hoffman and Kris Hampton

Power Company Climbing
Lander, Wyoming
www.powercompanyclimbing.com

Library of Congress Control Number: 2019919552
ISBN (paperback): 978-1-7341036-0-1
ISBN (ebook): 978-1-7341036-1-8

DISCLAIMER

Climbing and training for climbing are inherently dangerous. Your safety depends on your own judgment. The author, illustrator, and any persons associated with Power Company Climbing will assume no liability for accidents or injuries sustained by readers of this book. If you are unwilling to assume all responsibility for your own safety, please do not use this book.

**The impediment to action advances action.
What stands in the way becomes the way.**

-Marcus Aurelius

CONTENTS

FOREWORD	1
INTRODUCTION	3
IF YOU AREN'T MAKING PROGRESS, YOU'RE PROBABLY MAKING EXCUSES	7
CLIMB BETTER FASTER | THE MAGIC BULLET	9
TRAINING WHEELS | HOW TO CLIMB HARDER THAN THE OTHER NEWBS	13
THE CHAINS THAT BIND US	16
YESTERDAY I WENT SHOPPING. TALK IS STILL CHEAP	19
DON'T SQUASH THE BANANA | COMMITMENT	22
EVEN GOOD BETA SPRAY IS BAD BETA SPRAY	29
HOW YOUR FRIENDS ARE HOLDING YOU BACK	32
THE TOP 5 BAD GYM HABITS OF SPORT CLIMBERS	35
THE TOP 5 BAD GYM HABITS OF BOULDERERS	40
SANDBAGGED | ARE YOU KIDDING YOURSELF?	46
YOU SHOULD PROBABLY JUST TRY HARDER	49
YOU DIDN'T PUNT	51
TRAIN WRECK | 5 WAYS TO DERAIL YOUR TRAINING	54
YOU AREN'T ACTUALLY TRAINING	59

THE FALSE CEILING | HAS YOUR SKILL SET LIMITED YOUR TRAINING GAINS?	61
THE #1 REASON WHY YOUR TRAINING DOESN'T WORK	65
INTIMIDATED?	68
KEEPING PERSPECTIVE FOR THE WEEKEND WARRIOR	72
3 REASONS WHY SOFT GRADES MATTER	75
SUCCESS OR MASTERY?	78
THE SEND IS A NECESSARY PIECE OF THE PROCESS	81
NO KINGS, NO WAY	84
SELECTIVE LEARNING | THE SHORT-SIGHTED APPROACH	87
CLIMB BETTER FASTER | THE OFTEN-MISSING PIECE	89
GOALS NOT MET | FREEDOM AND TRANSWORLD DEPRAVITY	91
AFTERWORD	95
ACKNOWLEDGEMENTS	97

Foreword

By Katy Dannenberg

Years ago, Kris Hampton and I ended up in the same place at the same time: a resting ledge on the Motherlode wall in the Red River Gorge. Kris was attempting Transworld Depravity, which would be his first 5.14, and I was going up Flour Power on what was very much going to be a working burn.

I hadn't been in the climbing game that long, and certainly wasn't anyone to be giving any kind of climbing advice. Knowing the top of Transworld was soaked and Kris was going for it anyway (and at big risk of sounding cheesy, which stops me never) I called out to him, "You should snap the banana."

I remember Kris took a perplexed pause and simply said, "What?" I laughed and explained that I had just read one of his articles about commitment – the one about snapping a banana and if you don't commit, you get unpleasant banana mush. It was one of the most impressionable pieces on climbing training I had read at that point. I loved this: "You can plan every move you make. You can train harder and longer than anyone else. You might be the first person at the crag every day. None of it matters if you don't commit." Basically: "You can't half-ass it when you're banana snapping, or you end up with unappetizing mush."

So, there we were, two strangers trying to de-pump mid-route, talking about bananas and mush and what it would look like for both of us to go for it, all-in, against the odds, because why not? Why not give yourself the best chance to get a clean banana break instead of one of those moments we've all had in climbing – where you give the half-hearted go and immediately wonder why you didn't try just a little bit harder? The what-could-have-been moments.

And there we both were, with a chance for someone to hold the other accountable in a very banana-snapping moment.

Kris didn't send that day, but I don't believe it was for lack of commitment. In fact, I think exactly the opposite. The holds were impossibly wet on the top of Transworld, and so sending wasn't the indicator of whether the banana snapped or turned to mush. The way he dug in and went for it anyway, as if sending was still a magical possibility, was the coolest commitment I had seen. And the other part of that day that left such a lasting impression on me? While he was going for it up there, he took the time to keep cheering for me, a random girl giving a beta burn on a new route. I believe to this day that it speaks volumes to Kris's character and his love for the sport for all the right reasons.

Power Company Climbing has given me so much in the way of training advice, injury resolves, and hard truths; and I'm forever grateful for that Motherlode moment. I encourage all of you to find the glimmers of wisdom in this book that resonate with you because there sure are a lot of them. He will call you out and make you work for it because, as Kris says, "If you can't get psyched to train, then climbing harder isn't that important to you."

I hope you challenge yourself to snap that banana and that you have people around you who will step in and give encouraging reminders when you need to hear them most. Because if you've ever had a banana in your climbing pack, you know a squashed banana never did anyone any good.

-Katy Dannenberg

Introduction

Power Company Climbing began as a blog about an experiment. I was dissecting myself, working to figure out the best way to climb 5.14 by the time I turned 40. I wanted to be the best I could be within the parameters of my real life – career, parenting, homeowner, etc. I didn't have time for excuses, so I took a hard truth approach to every single session. No trophies for showing up. No medals for doing my job. No hollow back pats when the work I put in was half-assed.

Of course, that no bullshit approach made its way onto the blog. Those posts became some of our most popular. As not only The Power Company grew, but the climbing training community along with it, the messages in those essays seemed even more urgent.

A few things have changed with time. The girlfriend or fiancé in the essays is now my wife and we bought a house we love (and built The Machine Shop, our amazing home wall) in one of the best climbing towns in the country. While I now know that not every coaching situation calls for my no-frills approach, I still apply these ideas to my own climbing. In fact, I apply them to everything that I do, and I don't for a second consider that being hard on myself. Without mistakes, there's no reason to grow – but we need to acknowledge the mistakes before realizing the growth. I'm just quick to acknowledge the mistakes.

You may not be, and that's entirely ok.

I believe in the power of words to both help and to do harm. I'm aware that for some, the directness of the words chosen in this book may not be helpful. We are all on a timeline, and if these words impact you at the wrong time – while I can't apologize – I can suggest that you save them for when you might need them.

Some of the words used have changed from the original essays. My editor, Brittany, pointed out a few words and phrases that could easily be misinterpreted. We've worked hard to make sure the final words chosen are inclusive and better represent who I've become.

I believe in change. The necessity of it.

The entire purpose of this book is to push the boundaries of what's comfortable for you. To help you shine an uncompromising light on the nearly invisible aspects of your climbing that might be holding you back. I suggest you take a deep breath and use it for exactly that.

Maybe a few of these essays, some written over the years on the Power Company blog, some written specifically for this book – now paired with the brilliant illustrations from my friend Brendan Leonard – will resonate with you. Maybe they won't. However, if you've been a reader for a while, you already know that the reason you're feeling defensive is because I was looking right at you when I wrote this.

Incidentally, I didn't reach that dream goal of climbing 5.14 by 40. I missed it by three weeks. I blame that entirely on me.

-Kris

Planted on the ground, the act is so together.
Bonafide strong, you need leverage to sever.

-Q-Tip

If You Aren't Making Progress, You're Probably Making Excuses

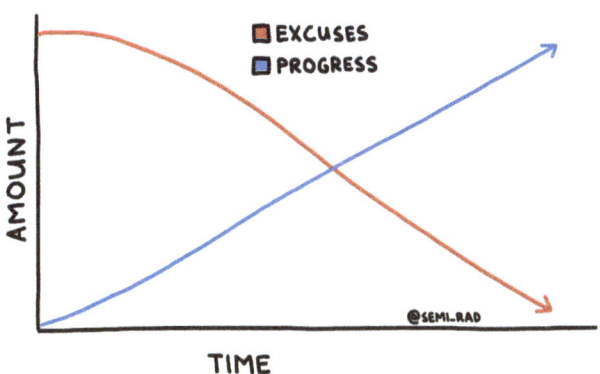

I hear them coming from every corner of the gym. From the mats beneath the boulder. From 30 feet up the lead wall. I hear them in the lobby before I even make it into the gym. No, not the voices in my head. Those are mostly quiet these days. What I hear are excuses. Tons of them. Never ending:

> "I'm too short. I wish my arms were longer."
> "I'm getting too old to climb hard."
> "I climb trad and that's harder anyway. 5.8 trad is at least as hard as 5.11 sport."
> "My schedule is just too crazy to have time to get stronger."
> "I climb for love. Training would kill that."

Blah, blah, blah.

Lynn Hill is 5'1".
Lee Sheftel sent his first 5.14 at the young age of 59.
5.8 is only as hard as 5.8 sport. Hence the number similarity.
I work 40+ hours a week (now running my own business), have a daughter (who's now having a daughter), built my own home gym, train hard, do house projects (with my wife, who also asks for some time), still find time to help cook dinner nearly every night and oh, would you look at that, I've made progress every season.

Please, tell me more of your excuses.

Fact is, we can all look a little deeper and find a few excuses that we're holding onto, and those excuses might just be holding us back.
My half crimp game is strong. My full crimp – not so much. For years I've been able to comfortably half crimp the grips that most people need to knuckle down on. I consider it a super strength. Recently I discovered a hold that I absolutely cannot half crimp. Everyone else at the boulder that day owned it – in a full crimp. I couldn't use it at all.
In this case, my super strength became a blinder. An excuse not to improve a glaring weakness. Have there been other times I could have done a move if I'd had access to a stronger full crimp? Positions I don't intuit because I have a hard time closing my hand on a small edge? I can't know for sure, but I know I'll have the full crimp in the arsenal next time around.
Even if you are making progress, look deep. Is there something you avoid? A hold type, an angle, a specific type of move? Anything? When people suggest you try that thing, what do you say?

Are you making excuses?

Climb Better Faster | The Magic Bullet

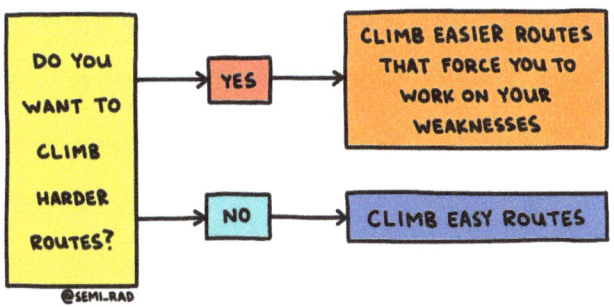

"What's the magic bullet?"

I get this question all the time. ALL the time. Mostly from beginners and climbers who can't seem to break out of the plateau they hit after doing what they always do has stopped working.

So how do you improve faster? There's a simple answer. You don't. That is, not unless you make some drastic changes and stop doing what you're doing, which essentially boils down to caring about climbing BETTER.

Just this week I was asked, "How do I climb harder problems?" My answer (I'm not the most understanding to dumb questions when I'm training) was, "Stop trying to climb hard problems." After the mix of embarrassment, hurt, and "Wow, this guy is an ass!" faded from his face, I offered one more bit of advice. "Spend your time in here learning HOW to climb. Climb the easier problems perfectly. All of them. After that, the next level will come easy."

Of course, he went right back to flailing on the first moves of every hard problem in sight.

My advice, of course, was specific to his situation. If you're a beginner, or if you're even relatively new and have been climbing less than two years or still don't regularly climb V4 or 5.11 (and by regularly I mean that you do it consistently – sending two V4s in the gym this month doesn't constitute consistently), then there really is a simple answer. You need mileage. Lots of it. Learn as many movements as you can. Stop spending all your time only trying to climb the hard problems in the gym. But that's an art in itself, so we'll save that for another time.

For those of you who are climbing 5.12 or 5.13 and have been at the same spot for several years, there really is a magic bullet.

A year ago, I would have told you that constant self-reevaluation was the bullet. I'd have been wrong. It's one thing to know that you're weak in an area, but it's another to work on it. To REALLY work on it.

Most of us evaluate ourselves regularly. We know we suck at slopers, so we gravitate toward crimps. Or we know we suck at steep, dynamic climbing, so we spend our time climbing tiny holds on a barely overhanging wall. We write detailed training plans, and then do whatever we feel like in the gym. We spend entire gym sessions telling everyone who will listen that we've decided to start working on focus and time management.

Good job continuing to suck at something.

The hard part is letting go of the ego involved and forcing yourself to work on those weaknesses. You might even have to do it in front of people. You may, God forbid, have to fall off of something beneath you. However, if you do it, and do it right, you'll enjoy a bit of the same growth you used to see every session.

Simple, right? Well, not exactly. Beware the simple path, for there are hidden dangers.

Don't go too hard.

There is a better time and way to learn these new skills. Learning new skills while under extreme stress isn't the way to go. If you're climbing V6 crimp ladders, but can't do a V2 compression problem, don't just throw yourself at a V6 sloper line. You'll teach your body even more bad habits by flailing all over. I'm sure I've used this analogy before, because I love it: professional baseball players don't always take batting practice with full speed pitching. The speed is reduced so that they can focus on the mechanics of the stance, the swing, and the follow-through. Start off working on your weaknesses on easy problems, where you can focus on really learning the techniques and subtleties involved.

Don't quit too soon.

Once you've successfully used a new technique, don't just assume you've mastered it and move on. You still suck at it. It takes thousands of repetitions to make a movement become automatic, and maybe more still to be able to see when to apply that new skill instead of the other hundreds of options. Keep at it. Forever.

Don't go too long.

Eventually your weakness can become your strength. It happened to me with local endurance, and it took way too long for me to realize it. I loved being the endurance monster in the gym, even though my power was pitiful. Be looking for it and switch it up before it happens. Constantly reevaluate!

Don't exclude your strengths.

No training plan that focuses on only one aspect of your sport is a balanced one. Spend time every session working on your weaknesses, but also spend time improving your strengths. There is no hard and fast ratio of strength to weakness that you should employ, rather you should feel it out for yourself. If you're having fun working on your weaknesses, do a little more. If your outdoor project is more like your strengths, do a little more of that.

Ignore the voices.

When you're in the middle of your training, and a group of guys is projecting something you've dialed in, ignore the desire to crush it casually in front of them. It isn't doing you any good, and it isn't doing them any good. Chances are, you were one of those guys. Or still are.

    This climbing thing isn't easy. If it were, it wouldn't be any fun. Frankly, part of the fun lies in the complexity of this beautiful sport. That complexity isn't easily solved, and there are far more facets than you can initially see. It can get overwhelming. Might as well start learning them now.

Training Wheels | How to Climb Harder Than the Other Newbs

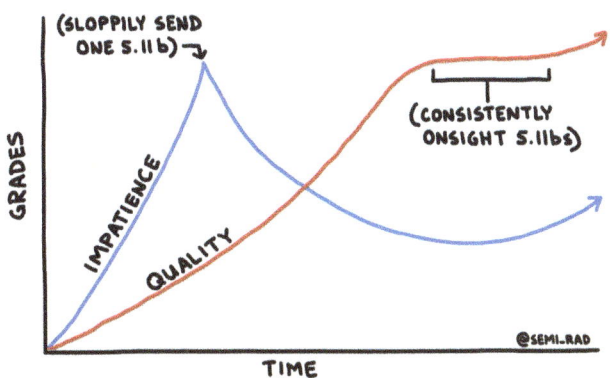

The blue line? This is you.

Yeah, yeah, I know. I was a newb once, too. But I'm not anymore, so I can make fun of you all I want. In all honesty, sometimes I envy your position. It was fun seeing massive gains every week. Now I fight for months to eke out half a letter grade (or less). Now that I think about it, you really DON'T want to get better faster. It's just setting you up for earlier obsession over training minutiae. And disappointment. Nah, forget it. Take up golf. Scratch that. Golf is even more depressing than climbing.

If you actually want to do this, I've already told you how:

Stop trying the harder problems.

Not altogether of course – but stop spending your entire well of energy throwing yourself at a problem that you know you look ridiculous on, just because it's a harder grade than your friend just struggled up.

Instead, put on the training wheels.

If I were you (and I once was), here's how my time in the gym would look until I could regularly onsight 11b and consistently climb V3 or V4 without jumping, campusing, whining, getting lucky, or my feet flailing around like an idiot:

1. Warm up for longer than you think you should on very easy climbs. Climb as smooth as possible. DO NOT adjust feet after looking away from them, blindly searching for a better part of the foothold. EVER. True, you have a point – Chris Sharma barely uses his feet sometimes. That's because he understands when that's the better option for him. When he does use his feet, you'll never see him blindly readjusting them.

2. Take three or four attempts at a route or spend 45-60 minutes on boulders – both that are a couple of letter grades above your flash level. These routes or problems should take five to eight attempts to send. Once you've sent, be sure to repeat them regularly. Getting better isn't a fluke, so don't be scared to ruin the feeling of sending something hard for you. Eventually, it will be a warm-up.

3. All other times – volume. Mileage. If you're sport climbing, link several easy climbs. Climb at every angle in the gym. Crimps. Slopers. Pockets. If you're bouldering, do ALL of the problems that are easier than your top flash grade. Try to do them perfectly. Then do them muscling through if you want to. Then again a different way. Mileage, mileage, MILEAGE! All these moves have to become automatic for you to access them at a moment's notice. Your bag of tricks can never be too big.

4. Two to three times a month, allow yourself a session to try something really hard. Get a glimpse of movement you can barely understand. When trying something this difficult, come up with your own solutions, but always pay close attention to how the better climbers do it, particularly those who appear to float through moves you can barely muster. Try to emulate their movement. Yes, I know that your way works for you. Try it their way, too. Why not get better at both methods?

In fact, this is roughly how my sessions were laid out until I could consistently onsight 12b, had redpointed 13b, and flashed V7. I might have waited a little too long to change things up. You won't make that mistake because I made it for you.

The temptation to get sucked into flailing with your friends will be constant. It might even happen that you won't send a specific problem as fast as your friends who don't take my advice. But you'll send all of the problems, and in style, not just that one. You'll be able to do them over and over. And a year or two down the road, when your friends are still only occasionally sending one problem of the grade, you'll have moved on to your very own, shiny, big kid bike!

The Chains That Bind Us

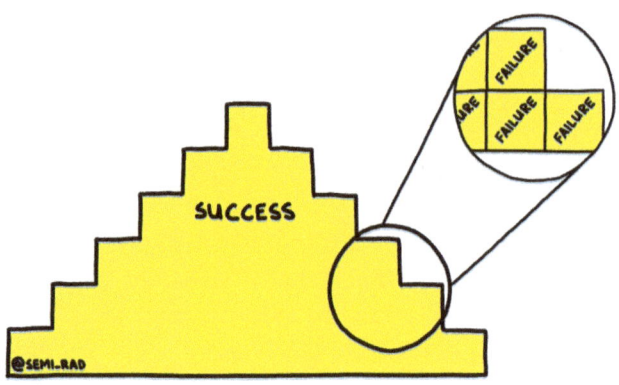

The top. The summit. The chains. No matter how you refer to it, success is often measured solely by whether or not you've sent. Fact is, seeing the chains as the sole representation of success is holding you back. And you.

And you.

Last Tuesday, I went to Red River with my friend and climbing partner Justin Riddell. We're both excited about training, about climbing, and, well, about sending. Justin had whittled his project, The Return of Darth Moll (13b) down to the point where it seemed the only progress to make was to send, and that was his goal for the day. As temperatures were still in the mid-high 80's, and my project, Swingline (13d), involves a few slopey, condition dependent crux holds, my goal was to try and onsight a 12d called Mind Meld.

The Return of Darth Moll, like most lines at the Darkside, is in your face from the first move, and doesn't let up until bolt #4, where it culminates in the crux move: hitting a finicky side-pull from a tension demanding under-cling, and unwinding out of it. On his first run of the day, Justin hit the side-pull, barely. He didn't quite get into the hold and wasn't able to make the tough transition out of it. However, it was progress, and he felt even closer to the goal of the day.

Up next, I planned my sequence on Mind Meld, taking note of thumb prints to determine the direction of pull on the temperamental pockets, making decisions about where to clip the scary 3rd bolt, and coming up with a plan B for the cruxy pocket section. I pulled on, climbed without hesitation, quickly found myself clipping the high 3rd bolt, and moved into territory I had misread from the ground. I had to really fight through a hard to read sequence, and with fingers opening, faced one last big move to what I assumed was a jug leading to easier climbing. I fell. My high right heel hook got in the way of my arm, stopping my momentum, and I just missed latching the jug.

Attempt #2: Justin knows it's close and is gunning for the chains. He climbs fast through the long intro sequence and just as he had planned, hits the move again. And is stuck. Again.

Attempt #3: After a short rest, and feeling ready, Justin fires up to the under-cling again. This time he hits the side-pull solid. And is stuck. Again. He digs in deeper, unwinds, and doesn't quite get to the next hold. Knowing he doesn't have the juice to try again, he continues up the unrelenting top to keep those moves fresh in his mind for next Tuesday.

No chains, no summit, no send. No parades or screaming, adoring fans. We both failed.

Or did we?

One of the beautiful things about rock climbing is that we're only pitted against ourselves. We'll never be stronger than the rock – it simply allows our passage from time to time. The real goal every time we get on a route or step up to a hangboard isn't to emerge victorious. It's to better ourselves. To improve. To find evidence that we're moving in the right direction. Justin stuck the move. A move that two years ago felt nearly impossible for him. Soon he'll stick the move, climb past it, and clip the chains that were his goal last week. Tuesday was progress. After twice freezing at the move, he was able to dig in and unwind toward the next hold. At the top, at the end of the day, he dug even deeper, and had to really convince himself to keep going. It worked and he now knows he can get through that section with little left in the tank. That's progress. Progress that will soon yield big results.

As for me? You either onsight or you don't. I didn't. However, there are a number of positives I can take away from the experience. Mind Meld is a far more bouldery route than I've ever onsighted at that level, and I nearly pulled it off. I moved confidently through the long bouldery section, never second guessing my planned sequence. I fought until total failure, pulling out tricks and staying patient, and it nearly got me there. Soon it will. My chance on this route is passed, but there are thousands more waiting, and Mind Meld was just a springboard.

Progress can come in small doses. Look for those little bits of improvement with every attempt. Something as small and subjective as feeling more comfortable on a foot smear can mean the difference between sending or not, so learn to be happy about every little tidbit you get.

I love clipping the chains just as much as you do. I also love the journey. Failure is what provides us the roadmap to that journey, and without it, we'll never see success.

Yesterday I Went Shopping. Talk is Still Cheap

True Story:

A kid at the crag wanted to try to flash a steep, cruxy 12b, which would have been his most impressive flash by far. The hardest moves are right off the ground and ease up considerably after the 2nd bolt, leading to a mostly juggy pump-fest to the chains. Standard protocol is to stick clip the 2nd bolt, where blowing the tough clip would certainly be disastrous. I gave the kid, who boulders stronger than I do, beta. Good beta. He climbed through the crux, and the very moment the 2nd bolt was at his waist he said "Take!"

Huh?

He then proceeded to go bolt-to-bolt to the top, looking shaky the whole way. After a rest, he tied in under a nearby 13a.
"Aren't you going to try the 12b again?" I asked.

"Nah, I'd just send it, so I'm going to move on."

Huh?

True Story:

A fairly new female climber at the crag wanted to try a pumpy 12b, which is at least a full number above her hardest redpoint. While the route has no real crux, and there is a great rest in the middle, it's a much harder proposition to link it all together than it might seem at first. She went bolt-to-bolt until she reached a slightly more difficult move just below the rest, which she immediately deemed too reachy (though the previous season I watched a 9-year-old warm up on it). After a few half-hearted abortive attempts, she retreated to the ground. Later I overheard her tell another girl, "that 12b isn't that hard, it's just reachy," and that "if it weren't for that move," she could have done it.

Huh?

True Story:

In every gym in this country there lurk sickeningly strong climbers who rarely touch real rock but crush seemingly impossible gym routes easily. If asked, and sometimes when they aren't asked, they will tell you that they COULD climb 5.14 or V12. It would be easy, actually, if they really wanted to.

Huh?

Now, it's certainly possible that the kid could have sent the 12b next go. It's feasible that, with time, the girl could find that pumpy 12 to be easy for her. And yes, it's likely that the gym monster could eventually climb those high numbers. The point is, they aren't doing it. They are just talking about it.

Talking is easier than doing. Saying you could do it is far easier on the ego than trying and failing. What it isn't, however, is nearly as satisfying. If you only talk and never subject yourself to the humility of failure, will you ever begin to know where your limits lie? I, for one, want to know. I put my goals out there and I try for them. Succeed or fail, I'll never have to feel regret that I didn't give it my all.

So, thanks to the doers. The people who get out and get it done. Thanks for the motivation, the inspiration, and for paving the way. Thanks for helping us to see that our own true story doesn't have to be a regretful one.

Don't Squash the Banana | Commitment

In the spring of 2011, while queued up beneath a 13d called Ultraperm, I witnessed the very definition of commitment. No, it wasn't someone skipping two bolts and risking a ground fall just to send. That would be stupid. Instead, it was an act so casual that it didn't catch the eye of any of the 16 other people waiting for their burn. My friend (and now Power Company Climbing coach) Nate Drolet, in line just in front of me, asked his belayer if she wanted half of his banana. Of course she did, who wouldn't? Rather than peel it and break it off with his chalky, dirty fingers, or dig in his pack for a knife, Nate – wait for it – snapped the banana in half. Clean break, right through the middle. Like a ninja.

My first attempt at snapping a banana ended in, well, banana pudding. It wasn't even a very ripe banana. Problem was that I didn't commit. I didn't go for it. I backed off at the last second. You can't half-ass it when you're banana snapping, or you end up with unappetizing mush. No bueno.

You can plan every move you make. You can train harder and longer than anyone else. You might be the first person at the crag every day. None of it matters if you don't commit.

It's not uncommon to see climbers squash the banana on a difficult onsight or redpoint attempt, and it's easy to spot. The climber gets to the crux move, looks up, looks down, looks up again, sometimes shakes their head no, and they're off. If your partner says, "Take!" in the middle of a redpoint attempt for no apparent reason, they might be a chronic banana squasher. It happens every day on tall boulder problems. These are the lapses in commitment that are readily apparent. This doesn't mean that they are easier to fix - just that you're more likely to get called out on them. It's the harder to spot lapses that are the most dangerous, and these generally follow a never-ending path paved with excuses.

I don't have the time.

If you've made this statement concerning training more than a handful of times in the last year, you are definitely squashing the banana. You and most other people. I'm sorry, but I have to call bullshit. More likely, the truth is that you can't bear the thought of missing out on time spent playing video games or watching YouTube to actually put in a little hard work.

You've got a lot to get done this week? Better get to it! I'd rather work a 60-hour week and climb on the weekend than stretch that work out over seven days.

Doing anything well will require sacrifice. If it comes so easy to you that you don't have to sacrifice anything then there is a good chance you aren't trying anywhere near your potential. If you're one of those people who think that you REALLY don't have time to do enough training to get strong, there are a few things to consider:

- Less time can mean more focused training. Throughout the majority of the year, my training time is only about eight hours a week. Five to six hours in the gym, over two or three small sessions, and an hour spent hangboarding in the early morning before work twice a week. You could easily get by with less, and if you have a small home wall, things get even easier. Four to five hours a week is plenty to make small gains, if it's focused (now that I have my own wall, six hours is about right for me). That means stop hanging out at the front desk or chatting the night away and get it done.

- You're probably training too much anyway. Systematic Work + Rest = Training. Without sufficient rest time, you are essentially moving backward. If you're in the gym five or six days a week, for several hours each session, get a hobby. One that doesn't require working out. If your muscles never get a chance to recover, how do you suppose they'll ever get stronger?

- While you're sitting here reading this book, there is someone out there, busier than you, training hard. Get your priorities in order and make a schedule. If getting better at climbing is a priority, then schedule it as such. When you learn to schedule around training time, rather than trying to fit training time into a busy schedule, you'll find that you're less stressed, more fit, and have far fewer excuses. If you keep it up, you won't need those excuses anyway.

- A tool as small as a hangboard can go a long way. If you really can't schedule any training time - you're absolutely maxed out - then get up an hour earlier and do a quick hangboard workout a few times a week. Hang while watching movies or between work calls. Finger strength is one of the cornerstones of climbing hard, and when not used, will disappear pretty quickly. You have room in your house for a small wooden hangboard, so build one and put it in. Otherwise, you're squashing the banana.

- Committing the time to get outside, particularly if you're a good distance from climbing, can be a little tougher. Again, the solution is planning. My friend Yasmeen and I, though we rarely climb together, start emailing plans on Monday for the following weekend. Changes and updates continue throughout the week, but by Thursday, I know where everyone I train is climbing for the weekend. Make plans. Make backup plans. Have a third option in case of Superstorm Sandy. Then stick to it.

I never even got to get on it.

Your day didn't go exactly as planned. Let me guess. You had every intention of getting on your hardest route yet, but a whole host of issues teamed up against you and kept you from it. You didn't bring enough food or water and felt hungry or dehydrated. It got dark too fast. Your skin hurt. Somebody was projecting it and hanging all over, and you just couldn't wait. You forgot your good shoes at home. You didn't get to bed until too late the night before. You forgot your coffee that morning.

Any other excuses you want to make?

- Add accountability. Tell your friends about your plan. Post it on Facebook. Mention it to your partners that day. Maybe then it won't be so easy to back out for ridiculous reasons. You'll have more people to answer to, and possibly more reason to go for it.

- Stop giving yourself excuses. This requires some planning ahead, but if you take care of your skin, you can't use it as an excuse. Pack your good shoes the night before. Never leave home without your coffee. Good preparation will leave you nearly excuse-less and will almost always leave you with a better chance to send.

- Make a list. For some people, checking off little boxes is a powerful reason to go do things. If it helps you, make a list, complete with little empty boxes. Hang it on your refrigerator or on your bulletin board at work.

- So, it's scary. Ok. I get butterflies in my stomach every time I step on stage and before most hard climbs. That isn't fear, it's anticipation. Once you step on the wall, let your training take over. The butterflies will disappear and soon there will be a great story to tell, whether you send or not. The only real failure is in never trying.

I just couldn't get psyched.

I'm not even going to legitimize this one with bullet points. If you need to seek outside your own self to find your motivation to rock climb, it's gonna be a rough ride. Maybe your partners weren't that psyched. Maybe they were moving too slow for your liking. Doesn't matter. It's up to you to set your own pace and make your own plan. It's great to have a psyched belayer, but a competent one will work just as well. Next time, look for partners who don't end every climbing day with a list of excuses longer than their brand new, never fallen on, 70-meter Maxim rope.

If you can't get psyched to train, then climbing harder isn't that important to you. Assuming that's the case, you should close this book and go hang out in the gym lobby. They are far friendlier than I am and won't tell you that you're lying to yourself.

I'm trying to get back in shape.

C'mon now. I've seen you in the gym every week for the last six years, and you've always been climbing at this level.
Forever. Exactly what shape are you trying to get back into? Maybe this only happens at my gym, but I doubt it. There are always a few people who are perpetually getting back into shape before they really start training hard and pushing into the next level. I understand. You've found your comfort zone, and it's hard to leave it. Do me a favor and try it a few times. Do it when the gym is empty, so there are no judgemental eyes on you. I bet you'll do something you didn't think you could, and you'll want to tell your friends about it. You might even want to spend a little more time on it to get better. Then again, maybe not. Comfort zones exist for lazy people. You should just stay there.

My elbows/shoulders/fingers/skin hurt too bad.

This isn't a new thing. You've been using the same excuse for six months now. Do something about it. Commit to the solution. Try everything you can to heal whatever problem it is you're having. If you had started when the pain did, you'd be fine now, you'd know how to remedy it next time, and you wouldn't have this excuse. Yes, I understand that the pain is real, but you're still at the crag or in the gym, so it isn't bad enough to stop you from climbing entirely. In fact, didn't I see you campusing problems in your flip flops with no warmup?

Uh huh. You get no sympathy. Do something to remedy the issue, or just shut up and push through.

Is it obvious that I just can't tolerate slackers for long? Here's my point:

If you don't commit to putting the time in, you'll never get the chance to have to commit to that crux move at the top of the hardest route you've tried. You'll never have the satisfaction of knowing that you pushed through the nerves and the fear, went for it, and took the fall. You'll never do that rockover move high above the pads and top out your first highball.

And that's perfectly ok, if you don't want those things. But if you do, I suggest you take a deep breath, commit, and don't squash the banana.

Even Good Beta Spray is Bad Beta Spray

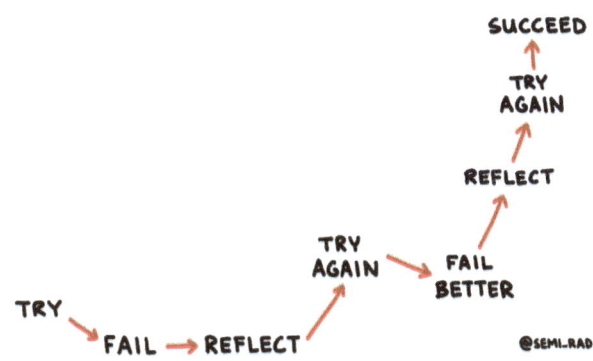

"For the things we have to learn before we can do them, we learn by doing them."
— *Aristotle*

Believe me, I understand the urge. You want to help. Or you want to show off. Or you want to be the resident expert. It could be that you have great intentions, and you really want to see that person succeed and progress in their climbing. I doubt it – but it's possible.

Problem is, progression is about learning, but because of your spray, they likely didn't learn a damned thing. The more I coach climbers, the more I become aware of this fact. I've been guilty. When one of my partners is struggling, I'm always happy to help them work out what beta will be best for them. I very rarely offer up beta to anyone other than my closest partners, though it's happened, I'm sure.

While I do try to always explain why the beta I'm suggesting is better, as well as my thought process in arriving at that conclusion, I'm still generally doing them a disservice by telling them in the first place.

Of course, there are two types of beta sprayers: those with good intentions, and those who just want to hear themselves sound smart. You know the latter. Ignore them. While the sprayers with good intentions might be more tolerable, they may also be harming you.

One of the most important parts of the learning process is reflection. It's been said that we don't learn from experience, we learn from reflecting on experience. Metacognition. Thinking about our thinking.

Too often we dole out beta that the climber isn't quite ready to understand. They might be three minutes from making the connection on their own or they might be three years from it. Regardless, if we give them that beta, and they can't sufficiently reflect on why it worked, what about it was better than the methods they had tried, and how to implement it further, then we've given them nothing. Less than nothing. We've set them back when they may have been so close to making the connection on their own and locking it down.

In my coaching sessions I still occasionally give beta. However, I now do it in a very specific way. I ask questions, or at most give positioning cues and tell the climber every step of my mental process in coming up with that beta and why I thought it would work. I work backwards with them from the point of failure – asking questions as we go – to find out what started the chain reaction that caused them to fall. More often than not, a week later I get a message saying, "I just used that new technique I learned to send a longtime project!"

If you're that person who gets flustered in five minutes and MUST ask for beta, then ask someone who can explain it and tell you why, rather than just tell you how they struggled up it as if there are no other options.

If you're the person giving the beta, the one with good intentions, take a second to decide if you're doing your friend a favor or depriving them of a valuable lesson, thereby stunting their growth.

Your partners and significant others are likely to get frustrated when they stop getting the beta that they used to rely so heavily on. However, in a season or two, they'll thank you for it.

How Your Friends Are Holding You Back

For as long as I can remember, I've witnessed a phenomenon at the gym that I've never been able to understand. Call it what you want: Social Abs, Core with Friends, Ab Circle, Club Core. I just call it mostly pointless.

Maybe that's unfair. Then again, maybe not. Fact is, in most cases, almost nobody in that situation gets any benefit at all from what they're doing. Unless, of course, the goal is to impress the strong girl leading Club Core with your circus tricks. That might work. Your climbing sure isn't doing it.

I'm not just ripping on the silliness I see in the gym. There actually is a point to this. Most of the people I see in the gym who are "training" are simply piggybacking off someone else's often misguided training program. People always want to know what my workout is that night so that they can do it too. It just won't work.

Let me explain it like this:

Let's say there are five guys and five girls in any given Ab Circle. Everyone is at least reasonably fit. Three of the guys are ripped, but they are the three worst male climbers. The two other guys and a couple of the girls are mostly social climbers and make no secret about it. Their climbing abilities range from about 5.10 to 12-, and from maybe V2 to V5. The other three girls are dedicated boulderers, at varying levels of skill. Everyone spends two or three hours climbing, then 30 or 40 minutes doing Social Abs flutter leg core exercises, followed by four or five participants (usually the less-skilled climbers) doing an hour or so of circus tricks, campusing, and chatting. They all do each exercise for the same amount of time, reps, and intensity levels.

Sounds fun. It might even be a decent workout. But as training, it's mostly worthless for all but a few of the people involved. I mean, ten individuals all doing the same workout in unison? It looks cute, but otherwise, pointless. Here's why:

The three guys who've worked hard to get ripped can probably handle a far more intense core workout than the less fit people, and it's unlikely to improve their climbing. They could have gotten much more out of spending time learning how to climb. The stronger climbers would probably get far more out of a sport specific core workout or from doing specific tension dependent problems. The people who are, by far, getting the most benefit from Core with Friends are the social climbers (the ones who care the least about getting better) and the physically weaker climbers. Not to mention, if you have the energy for post-workout campusing and yoga-style circus tricks, then your workout might be missing the point. If you're a regular in the Ab Circle, and it's difficult for you – good job.

My point extends beyond just end-of-session Circus Core. If you do the same problems in your 4x4 as your partner, then the two of you had better be uncommonly evenly matched. The same strengths and weaknesses. The same goals. Doing the exact same number of laps on the same routes as your belay partner means that most likely, one of you is trying much harder than the other.

Here's another common example: Two guys, Biff and Bam, always climb together and always work on the same problems. Biff sends after three or four tries then gets to sit and chat with the girls. Bam needs to refine his technique, dig deep for the power, and completes the problem after an hour of discovering a few new techniques. Unless Biff got a date out of it, which is unlikely, Bam wins. He may not be the better climber tonight, but he will be. Mark my words.

There is no single workout that any group of people can follow to get the optimum results for each of them. Doing your partner's workout just isn't what's best for you. You all have different ability levels, goals, drives, strengths, and weaknesses. If your goal is to get stronger, then your workouts must reflect your own individual needs. Not mine. Not your partner's. Not the other circus clowns.

The Top 5 Bad Gym Habits of Sport Climbers

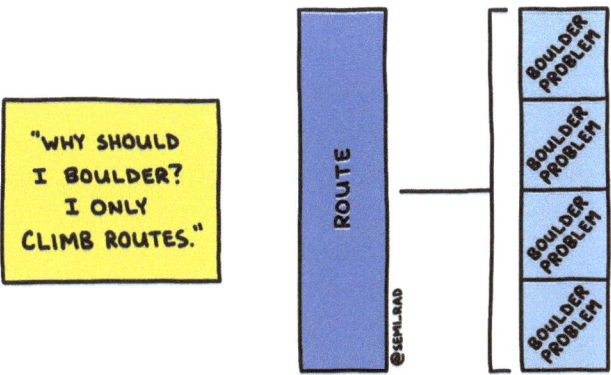

Originally here at The Power Company, we didn't often talk about the differences between climbers who choose to mostly climb routes and those who choose boulders. I'll go ahead and call that neglectful on my part because there are some fundamental things that are different about the two. We'll talk more about those differences in a later post, but for now I want to focus on a difference that wasn't obvious at first. The fact that while in the gym, for the most part, boulderers are closer than sport climbers to training the correct way. Since many people have a tendency to automatically jump to extremes to discount everything they read, let me note here that I said, "for the most part." You boulderers aren't off the hook.

To paraphrase several readers of Jaime Emerson's now defunct but excellent site, *B3 Bouldering*, "Why 5? Why not 10? Why not 20?" And to paraphrase Jaime's answer, "Because it's my book and my list."

Any more questions? Ok then, on with the show:

5. Going Climbing.

Let me start by saying this: if you go to the gym just to have fun with no desire to improve, then you should go and do exactly that. You should climb. Do whatever you want. Treat it the same way you do when you go outside. Just climb.

If you want to improve, however, you should definitely not go to the gym to just go climbing. If your goal is to treat the gym as training for climbing, then you'll have to structure it differently than you do your outdoor sessions. If your normal routine is to warm up, sample a few climbs, see how the project feels today, and then do three laps on the same 5.10, STOP. Do something different. Anything. Spend the night working on a project. Spend it on vertical top-ropes instead of leading the roof again. Go bouldering. And whatever you're doing – try hard. Learn something and take note of what you learned. This doesn't have to be an endless treadmill. If you do it right, it could get you somewhere.

4. Staying in Their Strengths.

When I look around the climbing gym, it's always the same people on the same angles. The crimp masters post up at the near vertical walls. The compression junkies find all the biggest slopers and stake out the aretes. Those opposed to footwork are campusing up the steeps. It never fails. Hooray, you did another 45 degree V9 sloper rig. Good job. But why do you keep telling people that the 15 degree techy balance problem is awkward and stupid? Because you suck at it, that's why.

Which is precisely why you should be doing it.

It's true, your hardest outdoor sends will likely be the ones that suit your strengths. However, the level of return you'll get on climbing solely at a particular angle or always on a particular grip will diminish rapidly. Paying closer attention to your weaknesses will make you a better climber. No question. And what happens when your ultimate compression project ends with a runout, techy headwall?

You'll wish you had spent more time on those awkward, stupid problems.

3. Counting Pitches, Discounting Quality.

Often when I ask sport climbers how their session was, I get an answer that details the number of pitches they climbed as if they're in direct competition with Alex Honnold or they're training for *24 Hours of Horseshoe Hell*. There's no mention of how hard they were trying, whether they learned anything new, or if they made progress on something. Only a confirmation that they reached their arbitrary number of scheduled pitches for the session.

Again, let me say this: if your goal in climbing is to get in a predetermined number of pitches each time you climb, and that is enough to make you happy, then by all means, keep doing it. I wish my goals were as simple to achieve. I envy you. However, if you want to improve at rock climbing, then somewhere along the line you got bamboozled into believing that a certain number of pitches is directly related to getting better. It isn't.

Well, that isn't entirely true. Sometimes it is directly related. When you are a beginner, or new to sport climbing, then it may very well be to your benefit to get in lots of pitches. If it's early in the season and you're getting your route legs back under you, I'll give you a pass. But if it happens every week, your pass is revoked.

Instead of concerning yourself with the number of pitches, try paying attention to the quality of the pitches, and the quality of the rest between pitches. If you're cramming 24 pitches into a three-hour session, it's likely that you aren't rested well enough to give 100% physically, mentally, or emotionally to your performance on 23 of those pitches. If the desire is to improve, I would rather see someone give three high quality attempts at a hard project or a climb that exploits their weaknesses than send 15 pitches at the same grade they've been climbing for the past five years. Quality, not quantity.

2. Take!

While I used to be a staunch traditionalist, I now see the truth. There is a time and a place for saying "take" and sitting on the rope. While working out moves. While warming up. For (actual) safety reasons.

There is also a time and place when "take" should be completely removed from your vocabulary. While in redpoint mode. While onsighting or flashing. While training.

If you're on a rope for training, it's likely that you're doing one of two things: a low intensity endurance workout in which you should never get near the point of failure, or a workout that requires reaching failure at a specific point to affect adaptation. In either case, unless for safety reasons, the word "take" has little place.

The gym isn't only a training ground for the physical aspects of climbing. For many of us, the gym is an important place to hone our mental and emotional skills. Learning to go for it in the gym can make for much more productive days outside. For the many of you who find that several days are spent on your project just convincing yourself to make the next move or clip, cultivating this skill while training can dramatically speed up the process.

Use "take" when appropriate, but when you've assessed the risks and you're ready to go hard? Forget the word entirely.

1. Ignoring Bouldering.

I used to be you. I "trained" solely on routes. I mean, I wasn't a boulderer, so why waste my time bouldering? Essentially, routes are a bunch of boulders all stacked on top of each other. Sometimes those boulders are stacked in your favor, sometimes they aren't. In every case, sending depends on how efficiently, if at all, you can do the moves. It all comes down to strength and power. If the hardest moves on a route are at your utmost limit, it's unlikely that you'll send, and the best way to get better at harder moves is to try them bouldering.

You can absolutely work on difficult moves on a rope. However, even if you've mastered the art of trying 100% despite the fall potential, you've climbed a number of moves just to get there. You'll use energy to pull back up the rope. It takes more effort. It takes more time. Stop wasting time and energy, and work on hard moves right on the ground. There is no better way to get stronger.

I've heard many sport climbers claim that they've never been shut down by a move, so there's no reason to train bouldering. Either you're abnormally strong, or you aren't trying routes that are difficult enough. I'd guess the latter. Even if you've never encountered a move that you can't do, gaining more power will make all those moves seem easier. You'll be less depleted for that last move showdown, or you'll have more left for the pump-fest following that first bolt nerd gate.

More power can't hurt. Less power certainly can.

The Top 5 Bad Gym Habits of Boulderers

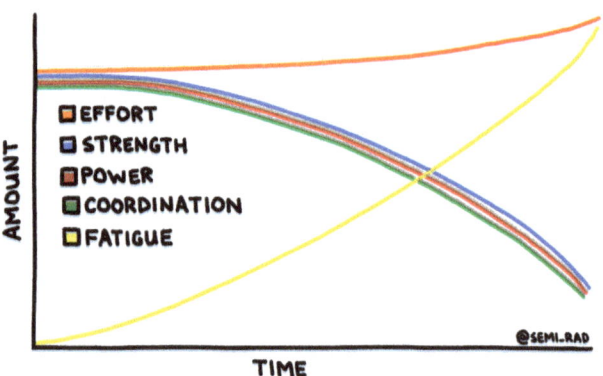

Years ago, when I was mainly a sport climber with big sport climbing goals, I wrote about the top mistakes I see other sport climbers making in the gym. Now that I'm mainly a boulderer with big bouldering goals, it's overdue that I point out the mistakes I see so many boulderers making.

See, told you that you weren't off the hook.

Honestly, I can't entirely lay the blame on you. I think all of these reasons stem from two things: the current commercial climbing gym culture and the inability of media to show what the full process looks like for the best climbers. We've discussed both of these things on the podcast on various episodes, and the more I pay attention, the worse it seems.

You might have good intentions, as do the gyms and the media, but frankly many of us are being slowed down by both of these things. Waiting for someone else to put your best interests first isn't going to get you anywhere. Instead, it's up to you to make sure you aren't falling into the traps.

The tools are at your disposal – it's all about how you choose to use them.

5. Too Hard for Too Long.

There is a time and place to do more, to go longer, to get exhausted. Most of the time, training to send hard boulders is not that place. At its core, bouldering is about trying to do the hardest moves and sequences possible, without the added complexity of ropes and widgets. It's rarely about determining how far you can push while fatigue sets in.

So why train that way?

There's a good reason that the grueling 1500m race is the final event of the Decathlon, which is widely considered the event that crowns the world's best athlete. Because if they started with the 1500, all of the more powerful events – 100m sprint, pole vault, high jump, etc. – would suck. We lose our top end strength and power when we're exhausted, and those energy systems are slower to recover. Coordination also drops with fatigue. Hard boulders require top end strength, power, and coordination.

This should be a no brainer.

Like I said, there is a time and place. If you can't determine that it makes perfect sense to keep trying until total failure, then don't do it. Even then, do it sparingly.

4. Always Projecting.

I once heard a climber say "Well, at least I can now say I'm working on V10!" I didn't see them do a single move or hold a single position on their new project. They barely even tried. For them, it was just cool to be projecting something hard.

By definition, a project is something that you aren't sending. Something that feels a little out of reach, or at best, you can see it in the distance. They are valuable. In my opinion, necessary. But there is one major issue with getting trapped in the obsessive projecting loop.

You aren't sending.

If you happen to be the particular brand of masochist I am, this may not be a huge problem, but for most of us, it's important to build momentum. The only way you can do that is by sending. If you only get to go on a bouldering trip for a few weeks of the year, it's absolutely imperative that you practice the skill of sending. And sending fast.

You certainly need the strength, power, and improved positional awareness that comes with limit bouldering and constant projecting, but don't underestimate the power of remembering how to send.

3. Ignoring Endurance.

Boulders are short, so obviously you don't need endurance, right?
Wrong.

I've seen enough climbers fall off of the relatively easy terrain after the crux of a 12 move boulder to know better. I've also seen plenty of climbers fade to dark after only a few attempts at a few boulders. Endurance and stamina are important if you want to send more than a single boulder a session, or more than the 4-move power test-piece.

This doesn't mean you should put all of your focus on endurance – just that you should reexamine why you believe it lacks value. Have you fallen off of a boulder because you're pumped? More than once? I figured as much.

Again, if you get a few weeks a year to try your projects – or if you're a road warrior who bounces from one area to another, putting in more high-quality efforts each day can be the difference between seeing your trip as a success or as wasted money.

A little endurance can go a long way and is too easy to come by to ignore.

2. Staying in the Middle.

This one I'm going to blame largely on the gyms, and it's dangerously close to my top reason why more people aren't climbing harder boulders. Let's look at the average gym climber and see if we can spot the error:

Miranda comes into the gym on Tuesday and sees that a new section of the boulder has been reset. She warms up on a few familiar problems and some of the new easy ones. Gradually she makes her way to the slightly harder boulders that she can get done in that session. One or two of them get away from her.

Thursday, she returns, excited to work on the problems that she didn't send on Tuesday. One of them goes down first attempt of the day, and the other takes some beta refinement before she tops it out. She finishes her session by sampling a few of the harder ones on the wall that she can almost conceive of.

The following Tuesday, Miranda shows up to the gym and sees that a new section of the boulder has been reset. She warms up on a few familiar problems and some of the new easy ones. Gradually she makes her way to the slightly harder boulders that she can get done in that session. One or two of them get away from her.

Sound familiar? It's a terrible cycle of staying at a middle intensity – never truly trying anything that is actually difficult – and one that many gyms perpetuate with their setting schedule. I GET IT. If I were running a commercial gym, I'd do the same. It's up to you to break the cycle.

Spray walls or set boards can be your best friend. Pick a project and maybe even ignore the new set for an extra week or two. You might not get to do every problem that you're capable of.

That's ok. Until now, you've essentially been ignoring the hardest boulders that you're capable of doing.

1. Not Enough Effort.

When I spoke with underground legend Brian Antheunisse on the podcast, he estimated that amount of effort given is where 99% of people are falling short.

I tend to agree.

To be completely honest, I want hard moves to feel easier than they are. I'm sure many of you do as well.

When we are learning to climb and progressing through the grades, it's often some should-have-been-obvious beta change, a subtle shift of the hips, or just a bit of learning the moves that makes all the difference between sending and not. That continues throughout this entire journey.

However, at some point when you've learned a lot about reading beta, or where your hips should be, at a point where the moves just get HARD – that little bit of learning might not do the trick anymore. It's frustrating as hell.

But how hard are you really trying?

Did you just expect it should feel easier after you tried it 15 times? Did you want it to flow more than it actually does? Are you just waiting to finally connect with it?

That's me. That's what I do.

It's been an all-out battle to learn to give 100% to a single move. It's not how I'm wired, but I'm making progress. Occasionally I'm able to summon everything I've got. Not often, but far more than I could a year ago. I've still got a long way to go.

How about you?

Sandbagged | Are You Kidding Yourself?

It's the new buzzword that's been around forever: sandbagged.

"That 10c is definitely more like 11b!"
"That CAN'T be 12a... I NEVER fall off of 12a!"
"This is WAY harder than the other two 13a's I've done, so it MUST be 13d! At least!"

Or more precisely...
"BLAH BLAH BLAH BLAH!"

Funny, I never hear, "Damn, that 10d kicked my ass. I guess I've got some things to learn," or, "That 13a felt pretty hard to me, I guess I should actually work on slopers for a while."

Nope. Instead, we blame the grades. The numbers. The proposed suggestions of vague measurement.

You're kidding yourself. Worse, you're stunting your growth. Holding yourself back. Even worse than that – if your friends believe your bullshit then you're holding them back as well.

First off, let's look at the word sandbagged. Actually, don't. Some of the definitions are a little crazy. Best to just leave those alone.

The two definitions I find most appropriate to climbing are these:

> *1. The act of undermining someone else's opinion subtly, yet in a public area, to make him/her appear foolish.*
> *2. When you're tricked into doing something because you weren't given all of the information you needed to make a good decision.*

Was the route graded low to intentionally make people look stupid? Doubtful. I, for one, have never seen it. Not in Vedauwoo, not in Joshua Tree, not in the VRG. The grades seem pretty much the same to me across every area I've climbed in. When they don't, I just assume I'm missing a key ingredient and I go back to the drawing board.

Were you tricked into something? Probably not. At least not directly. Maybe your gym's setters have an overinflated view of their abilities, or the V5/6 problems are closer to V3/4 – because the gym policy is to make the customers feel good. In which case, you go outside and THINK that you should be climbing V5/6. When you get shut down on that classic V4 that 30,938,349,087 people have done and reached a consensus on, you feel sandbagged, and you need to protect your ego by proclaiming it loudly.

I don't blame you. I sympathize (not really). But the grade isn't sandbagged. You were sandbagged by your gym. Blame them. Better yet, blame yourself for falling for it and putting so much weight in their proposed suggestions of a vague measurement.

Measurements that are faulty to begin with because your setters climb outside twice a year and say they get sandbagged on EVERY rock climb they try. See the pattern?

Bob Scarpelli, of Vedauwoo offwidth fame, is often considered by many to be the world's biggest sandbagger. Frankly, I didn't find his routes to be sandbagged at all. Did they feel ridiculously hard? Yes. Fuck, yes. But when I watched Bob climb them it became obvious that his technique was lightyears ahead of mine. As I learned from Bob and got better, the routes felt more like the given grade. Had I just blamed the grade I might never have gotten better at offwidth climbing.

When you're hanging there on the end of the rope or crumpled in a heap on your crash-pad, incensed that you've been sandbagged by this clearly under-graded rock climb, before you look foolish for voicing your thoughts, take a breath. This is an extremely valuable moment.

It's an opportunity to learn something. An opportunity to better yourself.

See, you have the tools to change yourself. You have gyms. You get to watch better climbers all day long if you wish. There are great coaches out there, (did I mention that we build machines?). You can get better. And best of all, you know EXACTLY what to work on.

You can also change that grade on your 8a scorecard, but you didn't get better as a result, did you?

You Should Probably Just Try Harder

How often do you give 100%? REALLY give 100%? I make my living coaching climbers and I seldom see a climber try their hardest. Myself included.

I like things to feel easy. I want it to look smooth. Effortless.

Not long ago I realized I hadn't had to fight for a single route the entire season. I chose routes that were easy enough to not require a battle, or I worked the more difficult ones into submission, until it was harder to make a mistake than it was to send.

I got soft.

Bouldering always felt hard for me. I could do V9 in a few tries, but not V10. Why?

I just wasn't trying hard enough.

I spent my next training season almost solely on an eight foot tall wall where all of my projects took maximum effort just to pick my ass up off the pads. Simply creating momentum was reason to celebrate but the hate-crimping required for every problem brought back the game face.

I sent three gym problems that season. Three. 15 total moves over 12 weeks. It hurt my fingers, and it hurt my feelings.

Those 15 moves asked more of me than any of the thousands of moves I had done on any route I had climbed.

A few weeks later, I sent my first V10. It didn't go perfectly. I had to battle. A few weeks later, I did another. Still another fight. I actually punched myself in the jaw during the top-out but that's another story. More followed.

Across the country, the season is imminent. The training you've done the past few months will be put to the test. While you're in the gym waiting for the weekend and that next time outside, I urge you to spend some time working on trying hard. Really hard. Are you giving 100% or are you dropping off because you didn't have the hold just right? Be honest with yourself.

It feels great to float something difficult, but it feels just as good to battle through errors, bad decisions, and failing fingers to find yourself standing on top.

You Didn't Punt

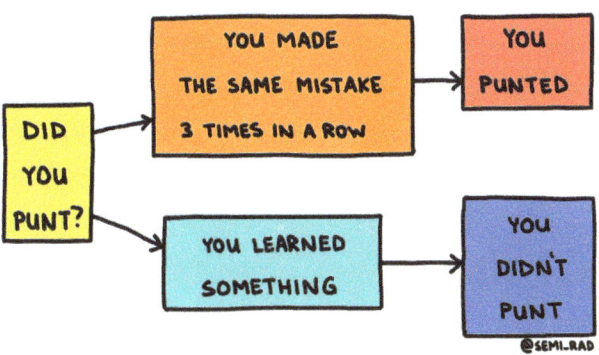

This essay doesn't exactly fit this book. On its surface, it's a simple lesson in semantics. I already told Brendan that he had everything that needed illustrating, and my project manager Brittany is going to tell me that it just won't fit into the flow of things. I don't care. I have to say it, and I think it goes deeper than semantics.

Sure, maybe you had the crux dialed in. It felt really good in isolation. And then you fell there. I'm not sure if you're aware, but that's where you're supposed to fall. It's why we call it the crux. The hard part. That's the point.

You didn't punt.

We came up with the term "redpoint crux" because it's another form of crux. A hard section when it's encountered starting from the ground, on redpoint. That's where you fell? I'm sure it is. That's the point.

You didn't punt.

Ok, maybe some of you actually don't know what the word means, or maybe you really do care about semantics. For you, we'll take a look at the word punt, as climbers have adopted it.

> punt2
> /pənt/
> verb
> verb: punt; 3rd person present: punts; past tense: punted; past participle: punted; gerund or present participle: punting
> 1.
> AMERICAN FOOTBALL
> kick (the ball) after it is dropped from the hands and before it reaches the ground.
> "he used to be able to punt a football farther than anyone"
> (of an offensive team) turn possession over to the defensive team by punting the ball after failing to make a first down.
> "the Raiders could get nowhere with their possession, and had to punt"

Notice the last usage here. "*Turn possession over to the defensive team.*" When you're on a redpoint attempt, you are the offense. The route is the defense. You don't get to where you need to be, so you're forced to turn the ball over. To punt.

But it's not that simple.

If you make the same mistake two or three times, you punted. If you get to the easy section that you rehearsed over and over and fell because you got excited and went to the wrong hold, you punted. But some falls – some failures – aren't punts. They're necessary.

Redpointing is a process. It's an ultimate success built on the backs of many failures. Oftentimes those failures are exactly where we are supposed to be.

So you climbed through the crux, which you worked at length, and then wasted energy through the next sequential section, only to fall at the redpoint crux?

That's exactly where you're supposed to be. You got your first down. You moved the ball. You learned something. Now you get to try again.

You didn't punt.

Train Wreck | 5 Ways to Derail Your Training

Training isn't all about success. In fact, much of it is about failure. Hell, climbing is all about failure. It's what success is built on. However, failure to make progress within your training, over time, is exactly that... a failure. Maybe that's a bit harsh; we'll call it a setback, since you have every opportunity to reevaluate and move it forward.

    We all, at some time or another, will have to face the reality that we just aren't getting better as quickly as we like. It's that realization that should force you to take a step back and try and determine where you've taken a wrong turn. These little detours aren't always so easy to spot, as up to now, it's obviously worked for you. Not any longer.

    There are thousands of ways that your training can be rendered ineffective or inefficient. I'm assuming if you've gotten to the point of reading this book, you've successfully run the gauntlet through at least several hundred of those ways. Discovering the sticking point is now much more difficult. After much deliberation over a list of about 25, I've decided on the top 5 ways I see experienced climbers derail their progression.

5. Ego.

This one is especially hard to avoid. Let me first say that I believe ego to be a positive motivator when used with boundaries. It's when out of bounds that ego becomes dangerous, and can manifest in a number of ways, including leading you directly into several other of the top derailers. Just a few examples you've all seen or experienced:

The new girl (or guy) at the gym is working on a steep juggy problem, so you feel the need to go send the V7 you have dialed right in front of her. Then the V8. Then you downclimb the problem she's working on. And back up it. Now you're pumped AND stupid.

Your training focus is on anaerobic endurance, and just before you begin your 4x4's, all of your friends are having a campus session. You know you're closer to doing 1-5-8 than they are, so you join in. You never get 1-5-8, and now you're too powered down to even complete one set of the 4x4 you've been closing in on.

You're focused on bouldering for power, but a new purple with cheetah print project has gone up on the lead wall and out the roof. At 12+, you could onsight it AND get the first ascent. You fall at the end, blow the onsight, and get pumped silly, which ruins your power session for the night.

Dumb.

4. Performing Too Soon.

Number 4 is sneaky. Good temps can lure you in with barely a whisper, and two weeks later you're back to square one.

The scenario:

You've trained hard and smart the entire off-season. A month before your training cycle is complete, the humidity drops, the temps become prime, and unexpectedly, the season has arrived! You're out the door to the crag and putting in early work on the project. You decide to skip your workouts in favor of saving energy for the real thing. Next week, the temps are holding, and you're making redpoint attempts. A week later, as if it never happened, the temps are back to scorching. Humidity is at 80%. You didn't send. Back in the gym you can barely even send your previous warmups. All of your hard-earned power disappeared with the weather window.

When the real season begins, will you be ready?

3. Copycat.

I see this one often enough to find it alarming. I also often hear people defend their training choice by citing this common training mistake.

> *"Well, it works for Bill Ramsey."*
> *"Sharma doesn't train."*
> *"Patxi trains every day, why can't I?"*

I could be wrong, but there is a good chance that you aren't, and never will be, Bill Ramsey, Chris Sharma, or Patxi Usobiaga. Just a guess. Ramsey and Patxi's training would maim the average human, and Sharma's style of training would strand most of us right where we are – if not below. You also aren't me, so you shouldn't do exactly what I do. You aren't the strong girl at your gym, so why mimic her workout? Smart climbers adapt their training methods to fit their strengths, weaknesses, available time, level of commitment, etc., etc., and so on and so on. Essentially, you have to determine what is best for your training, and chances are that it won't be the thing that sounds the most fun to you.

Just to paint the picture:

You read Bill Ramsey's workout online, and it immediately sparks your interest.
　　"I love getting crazy pumped while I work out! I love pullups! I love working out ALL THE TIME! This is definitely for me!"

Sure it is, if you're Bill Ramsey. Here's the difference: you've now been doing this workout for two months, and you still can't boulder V4. Bill could boulder V6 in his sleep long before he did 47 million treadwall laps. It's true, you now have amazing endurance. As long as the moves are V1 or easier, you're money. Fantastic.

2. Doing the Same Ol'.

Most people I know, myself included, are easy prey to this trap. If it's been working, why fix it? "Campusing and limit bouldering have worked for me for years, why on earth would I do 4x4's?" The short answer - because you want to get better. This isn't rocket science. As you progress, your returns on the same workout will diminish. No question.

In this same camp are the climbers who only work on their strengths, while never attacking the weaknesses that limit them. It's the same thing, week after week, season after season. Even if you began working on your weakness, and never reevaluated, there's a good chance that it's become a strength, and you're now stuck in this rut.

Eventually both of you will be left searching for the routes or problems that best suit you rather than improving your skills to make harder routes or problems possible. That's a sad moment, because it means that you believe you've reached your physical limit. Or, maybe you have reached it, and you feel enlightened to have realized it. Better you than me.

1. No Plan.

I'm amazed by the people who come into the gym to train with barely a vague idea of what they are going to do. On Tuesday, they do a 4x4. Thursday, some campusing. Saturday, a little bouldering and an off-the-cuff core workout. Maybe some Core with Friends. Many of these people record their results in some sort of journal, but without a control, and so many independent variables, what exactly is the data telling them? I'm guessing that it tells them whatever they want to see in it.

I'm all for training by feel. It's my preferred way of navigating most of life. Regardless, I have to be honest about the fact that all of this training we do is an experiment, and without a controlled variable, there essentially is no experiment. You can't possibly know what caused you to perform better in a given season if every step of the process is an independent variable. You can think you know, but you'll have no data to back that feel up.

Me, I've got a plan, and I'm sticking to it.

You Aren't Actually Training

Training is extra popular right now. Everybody and their mom want to train, has training advice, and can give you a three minute video depicting their training. This may sound like a plus, particularly for someone who sells training programs, but that isn't necessarily the case. Just take a look at your Instagram feed. Click on the first training video you come across and you'll find 27 comments from people tagging their friends.

"We HAVE to do this!"

No, you don't.

It's a good bet that it won't help you at all or, if it does, it's only because you're so untrained that you'd probably get that much stronger just by watching *Cliffhanger*. You already know my thoughts on doing the same workouts as your friends, so we don't need to go into that.

What you want to do is workout. This isn't training. Two totally different animals.

Semantics, you say. Blah blah blah. But, for me, these are important semantics. So, what's the difference?

Working out is essentially the pursuit of being tired, with sweaty clothes and next day soreness. It's unlikely that simply working out will make you much better, because it lacks direction and specificity.

Training is a series of progressive, measurable workouts that move toward a clear set of goals. Training takes into account the strengths and weaknesses of the individual athlete and stays specific to the needs of that individual athlete.

Not the same.

Now, to play devil's advocate – it's possible that the workout video you're watching is exactly what you need. Doubtful, but possible. However, nine times out of ten, most people don't have a clue what they need, so every workout video, even when they contradict each other, is the RIGHT one.

This isn't to say that working out is bad and I'm not saying that these videos aren't useful. They give a glimpse into how the pros work out, which is interesting to see. For me, they give an idea of how much further climbing can go when smarter training finally takes hold. And frankly, most of you could use a workout or two.

Just keep in mind that you can't do "a little training." You can't go into the gym and "train a few times before the road trip." It doesn't work that way. Training takes thought, diligence, and dedication. Working out can happen spur of the moment but training requires planning and sacrifice. There are plenty of ways to train even if you don't know how to get started. Talk to someone you know who has a track record. Hire a coach. Check out one of our Proven Plans. And finally, really pay attention and learn to put your ego aside to self-evaluate or take criticism.

Or just go work out. There's no shame in that. Just stop telling everyone that you're training.

The False Ceiling | Has Your Skill Set Limited Your Training Gains?

Several years ago, I came off a hiatus to rediscover rock climbing, in the form of clipping bolts. After embarrassingly realizing complete failure on an 11a (and an incredibly painful pump that lasted about six hours) it was obvious that I lacked endurance, specifically when the rock was even slightly steeper than vertical. Like any good climber, I got my ass into the gym asap and ran laps like a madman. Up, down, up, down, up, down again. Soon I was an endurance machine. 5.12 went down without a fight. 12d seemed tough, so I spent a week in the gym working on anaerobic endurance on pockets, and I went back out and did 12d, twice, back to back. My first 5.13 took four tries. I was cruising along, thinking that 5.14 must be just around the corner. But right about the time I hit 13b, I hit something else as well – a false ceiling. I trained harder than ever. No improvement. Still harder. No improvement. Harder again. Burnout.

Why couldn't I get stronger?

More than once I made the comment, "Who needs power when you have technique?"

How wrong I was.

This false ceiling I had bumped into was all about a lack of power and the techniques associated with it. Without that extra power, my anaerobic endurance was absolutely maxed and could go no higher. I had upped the intensity, but the workout had basically stayed the same and my body needed something different to respond to.

If you've been stuck at a specific difficulty for some time, you may think that you're nearing your genetic potential. Oftentimes, this is far from the case. Reaching genetic potential isn't as easy as destroying yourself at every training session and hoping that it transfers to the rock. Examine your training. Has it gone through any dramatic changes in the last year or two, or have you, like so many others, succumbed to the trap of repeating a familiar workout ad nauseum?

Let me say this: if you have a glaring weakness, consider yourself lucky. Realizing that my power was a major weak link was the last easy conclusion I've come to regarding my training. When the weaknesses are harder to locate, the decisions about how to train become infinitely harder, and the improvements miniscule. Count your blessings and let's look at your weakness and at how you're training.

Here's how it usually plays out:

You discovered some unique training tool or workout that sounded like exactly what you needed. After a few weeks of use, you saw great results. You kept with it and reaped the benefits for months. Then the results tapered off. Every time you were getting flustered at making little progress on the rock you would just flog yourself harder in the gym. When you were about to drop the workout, you found some small reason to keep doing it. And on it goes.

Stop. Now.

Open your eyes and look very closely at your climbing. No excuses. No saying, "Oh, that's just how I climb." No citing that one time you tried to use the sloper instead of the crimp and it didn't work. Just an honest evaluation. In the past year have you talked about a weakness repeatedly, but not addressed it in the gym? We all know what we're bad at. We just generally push it to the back of our mind, and keep building on our strengths, with little or no improvements in overall ability. Pull that thing, or things, out of that dusty corner, brush off the cobwebs, and make it your main focus for the next phase of your training. Take those training tools that you've been using and turn your back on them for the next few months. If you always do laps? Go bouldering. If you always boulder? Run some laps.
And on and on and on.

Yes, you.

Maybe I'm beating a dead horse here, but I'll say it again.

Most climbers I talk to have some excuse as to why they aren't training their weakness. Many of their workouts are the same, every week, year after year. They talk, read, eat, and breathe training and climbing, but rarely make the necessary changes to their training to stimulate their body.

The fact is, you WILL NEVER get within earshot of your potential if you don't have a complete skill set. No matter how hard you train, no matter how much blood, sweat, and tears you contribute to the cause, you'll never get the job done without the tools. So, what are you waiting for?

I understand. It's scary. It's a blow to the ego to go into the gym and really suck in front of everybody, or even just in your own head.

But how comforting is it to watch other climbers keep passing you up?

Train smarter, not harder. And when you learn that?

Train smarter AND harder.

The #1 Reason Why Your Training Doesn't Work

Do as I say, not as I do.

    I wish those instructions actually worked, but they never do. Fact is, I train hard. I train smart. Most of the people I work with do the same and I'm not shy about telling them that if they are taking shortcuts, they are only hurting themselves. But here's where it goes wrong – wrong for them, but right for me, that is. I choose not to climb outside when the conditions aren't good.
    At 90 degrees F with 90% humidity, I'm going to stay in the gym. EVERY. SINGLE. TIME.
    That doesn't mean that it's right for you. More than likely, it isn't. Most of the people I work with have only been climbing seriously for a few years and they all stand to gain a wealth of experience by grinding through the heat of a summer or suffering through snowy, freezing days. I've climbed thousands of routes outside in every condition imaginable; they've climbed 30 or 40 routes TOTAL.

You CANNOT shortcut experience and you don't get outdoor climbing experience in the gym.

I see it over and over again:

A climber trains hard all summer long, never touching rock until the prime season arrives. They go outside for ONE day and send me a frantic email on the way home.

"It didn't work!!!! I fell on a 5.10!!!! I can't believe it – I trained so hard but I got WEAKER!!"

It takes me a minimum of a few routes to get back into real rock mode. That's after thousands of routes of every style - slabs, faces, steep caves, roofs, cracks, corners, roof cracks, off-widths, chimneys, sport, trad, runout scary headpoints, etc. etc.

You've got 40 routes under your belt? Expect about four or five days AT LEAST before you get comfortable, and that's only if you've ever been comfortable to begin with, and if those four or five days happen in the span of a couple of weeks.

40 routes on your all-time tick-list and you only climb outside twice a month? Expect to spend half of your season getting comfortable. In fact, you shouldn't have a "season", you should just go climbing EVERY CHANCE YOU GET ALL YEAR LONG.

Put simply, the wider the base of your pyramid, the less chance it has of toppling over.

I know lots of 5.12 and even 5.13 climbers who skip the less than desirable days, and because they are climbing 5.12 or 5.13, it seems they've been successful anyway. Not so. It's not uncommon for those climbers to spend their first two or three attempts on a route just getting the jitters out. Let's say those two or three attempts take up a whole day – which isn't a stretch. Over the course of a season, even if you're the type that sits around most of the day, that's at least 10-12 attempts.

That's five or six days of prime temps that you've WASTED. Here are the facts. No amount of training will make you comfortable in a performance. Not for a job, not for a musical, not for climbing. You MUST spend time in the actual arena to become comfortable in that arena. There are no shortcuts.

When it comes to finding the right zone, experience trumps training. Every time.

You know that girl who never trains but always seems to out climb you, without even trying hard? The one you burn off in the gym and spray beta at because your ego demands you assert your dominance? You know why you don't see her in the gym on the weekends during the training season? It's because she's outside, getting experience.

You're getting stronger, but she's getting better.

God forbid she discovers training! Your poor little ego wouldn't stand a chance.

Intimidated?

Our egos are ruthless. Whether we want them to be or not, they are always there hiding just beneath the surface ready to throw a wrench in the works. I recently spoke with a climber who was feeling, for the first time ever, competitive about his climbing. I've seen climbers stop a session early because they, admittedly, didn't want to look bad by failing on a 5.11 in front of people. Years ago at Rocktown, a popular bouldering area in Georgia, I encountered it myself, for the first time in quite a while.

The day started off strong, having onsighted a V5 while warming up and sending my V8 project, The Vagina, in a just a few attempts. I figured that with temps nearing perfection now would be the time to go check out my ultimate dream boulder, Golden Harvest (V10). As I approached the boulder from the backside, I could hear voices, and strangely, found myself hoping that the climbers were working on the V5 next to Golden Harvest.

They weren't.

There were three guys working on Golden Harvest, and according to the incessant spray, they were all close to sending. They looked strong. They were obviously dedicated boulderers, while I toted around a pad older than their climbing careers. I took a little time to commit, not wanting to make a fool of myself by falling off the first moves, which from the looks of things, were quite difficult.

After watching several attempts from the climbers, and taking a deep breath, I found myself standing at the start holds of one of the most beautiful boulders in the Southeast. I had watched the beta intently, visualized myself making the first couple moves, and stepped on without hesitation. To my surprise, the (what had appeared to be difficult) first move went easily. I almost hesitated on the second move, thinking that I must be doing something wrong for it to feel this doable. On my first try, I was able to get set up for the crux move and move toward the distant, hard-to-snag hold. I was nowhere even close to hitting it but, on that first attempt, I had equaled the high point of these "stronger" climbers and more importantly, had vanquished the jitters.

While sitting there on my ancient pad, psyching up to commit to trying, I had a few important thoughts. Regardless of the outcome, the situation was going to end up a positive one. Here's why:

Playing it Safe is the Biggest Risk of All.

How many times have you returned home from a climbing trip only to say to yourself, "Damn, I should have at least TRIED it while I was there"? The cost of missed opportunities is far greater than what you pay for the attempt. In my case, it was important for me just to try the boulder. I had admired it many times, and many times had passed on the opportunity, wondering what it would take to climb it. Now I have a much better idea.

Trick Yourself into Believing.

The human psyche is a complex thing. If you don't believe something, you can't just tell yourself to believe it, and *POOF!*, it's done. While it isn't necessarily a "trick", you do have to find creative ways to convince yourself to believe. Because it isn't steep, and the holds are sloping side-pulls and odd under-clings, it became immediately clear that Golden Harvest is all about balance, body position, and subtle movement. If I had to rank my climbing skills, those three would be at the top of the list. Also, while watching, one of the climbers, the most vocal of the group, claimed to have gotten a foot not quite right, though it appeared to me to be a straightforward foot cam that any crack climber would own. This boulder was mine for the taking.

Throw Your Hat Over the Fence.

My grandfather always told me that if you want to climb the fence, but can't muster the courage, throw your hat over. Now you've got to climb the damn thing, or the hat is lost forever. For me, it makes me work harder if I announce my intentions. When the guys asked me if I wanted to try the problem, I responded, "Someday I'm going to do it, so I may as well try it today." Sometimes I talk without thinking, and maybe over-confidently, but it's worked for me so far. I had already told my friends I was going to check it out, and now I had told these guys. At that point, there isn't much choice but to give it a go. More often than not, I'm glad I speak up.

When in Doubt, Remember the Ewoks.

I'm not a *Star Wars* nerd by choice, but by default. Two roommates of mine in a row knew more about the stories than George Lucas. I've lost more games of Star Wars Trivial Pursuit than I can count. Now there are stories in the films that I constantly refer to. One of these is the Ewoks. Originally, Lucas had Wookies in mind for the battle with the Empire. He wanted to highlight the idea that simplicity could overpower technology, so he created a new species, the primitive and less intimidating Ewok, to fight (and beat) the Empire.

I'm also not a full-fledged boulderer, but I've become part boulderer by necessity. No, I didn't have the latest crash pad or a brand-new chalk pot. I still climbed more like a sport climber than a boulderer. I hadn't done a single V10, and only one V9, while these guys sprayed about their packed tick lists. In short, I was intimidated. Once I took a minute to remember that my training and my skills were what I had to fall back on, and that the only competition was between Golden Harvest and I, all of what I wasn't didn't seem to matter so much.

What mattered is what I am, and that I was standing exactly where I wanted to be.

Keeping Perspective for the Weekend Warrior

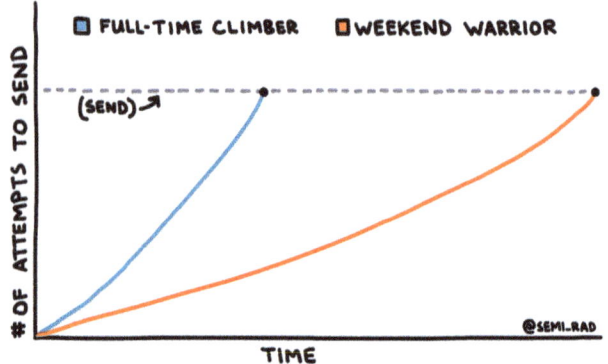

I feel your pain. It's easy to get discouraged by how quickly the pros seem to put down the hardest projects, when for two seasons you've worked on the same 12c, and still haven't been able to clip the chains. Maybe you're just in too far over your head? Maybe those guys and girls you read about just aren't trying things that are hard enough for them?

Maybe. But probably not. I'll use myself as the example here:

In the spring of 2010, I took my first run up what was, at that time, the hardest route I'd been on, Swingline (13d). It was simply a "free feel" as I like to call it, as I had sent my project for the day. It was my one foray up it for the season and I continued with the sending spree I was on, completing ten new 5.13's, including some of the hardest 13b's in the Red.

The following season, autumn of 2010, I dedicated mostly to Swingline to no avail. That season I sent only two new 13's and, in my mind, it bordered on wasted. An entire season of warm but mostly good weather and I just couldn't get it done. Skin issues, bad tactics, whatever. At this point, I had probably been up this damned route 35 times – eight or nine times to the final crux and what was now "the move." Fail.

Spring of 2011, I made the decision to not lose a season to one route. I dedicated the bulk of my time to other routes, completing a 13c, my first 13d, and a couple of 13a's, as well as doing my first "not in my backyard" 13c that July in Lander, Wyoming. I did visit Swingline a handful of times, raising the attempt tally to somewhere in the neighborhood of 40.

Autumn 2011, while mostly a wash for me due to remodeling a house, did provide a few more days to fall off of Swingline. Perhaps ten more tries, and I'd officially been working on this route for a year.

Spring of 2012 came quickly but I finally felt prepared for Swingline. Out of the gate, I spent most of my time on the famed Gold Coast wall, working on a route that routinely gets destroyed by 10-year-olds, God's Own Stone. When temperatures warmed, I managed quick ascents of Dracula '04 and Cat's Demise, two of the Red's best and hardest 13b's. In one of my best climbing days ever, I warmed up on The Force (13a), casually sending it twice, fell at the high crux of Swingline four times, and then finished the day with a surprise 2nd go send of Second Nature (13a). It seemed the fitness was there, but I just couldn't make it happen. As summer neared and my fitness dwindled, I discovered new beta that transformed "the move" from a desperate drive-by to a 1/4 pad two-finger pocket, into a totally static, can't fall move. I didn't get there again that season.

Shit! Did I blow it? Did I let the chance pass me by? I finished the season with my first 13a flash, and by doing two 13a's and a 13b over the course of four days in Lander. My fitness was still good. What the hell happened?? At this point, I was definitely pushing 60 on the attempt-o-meter and looking at two years of being thwarted by a single route.

Autumn, 2012. Knowing it would be too warm early in the season, I spent my time cleaning up a few routes I had tried but never finished. One 13a, one 13b, a 13c, and some work on a couple of 13d's, and the temps were getting good. On a particularly cold day in November, with the try tally hitting around 70, with only my small crew at the wall, I finally clipped the chains.

Two years.

The media reported that Adam Ondra only took nine weeks to send La Dura Dura, the then hardest sport route on earth.

Nine weeks spread over two years, that is.

Adam Ondra is a full-time professional climber. Arguably the best in the world. In his own words concerning the length of his La Dura Dura campaign:

"70 tries could be somewhere close to the truth."

Thanks Adam, for helping me keep it in perspective.

3 Reasons Why Soft Grades Matter

I'll come clean – I'm a defender of soft grades. In my opinion, they not only matter but they are necessary for growth and balance. Does that mean I'm against stiff grades? Not at all. In fact, if we didn't have soft grades wouldn't stiff grades just be your average everyday normal grades?

Honestly, I'm bothered a little every time that I hear someone disparage or choose not to do a certain climb because it's considered soft. I should just let the ridiculousness of it float away in the breeze but it's a tough one for me to let go of for whatever reason. I feel the same defensiveness when Sierra Blair-Coyle is dissed, but that's a different story for another day.

Here is a fact for you:

When you do a rock climb and log it on your 8a, no matter what grade you give it, or what grade the guidebook gives it, the difficulty of said rock climb does not change. It's exactly the same amount of challenging for you no matter what number you, or anyone else, attaches to it.

Hard to argue, right? So let's talk some of the reasons why soft grades should remain exactly what they are:

1. Progress

For the sake of progress, we need soft grades. The next logical step from a stout 12a is still a soft 12b no matter what your ego wants to do. I've seen dozens of climbers spend months adding half pound weights to each successive hangboard workout and then want to jump to the next stout grade when they get outside. Why throw out the logical progression when your time is limited, and it matters most? Is your ego controlling things?

2. Quality

You know what? Some of those butter soft 12b's are *REALLY FUCKING GOOD*.
  Some of those super stout 12b's *REALLY FUCKING SUCK*.
  Frankly, I'll take a 5-star inflated V7 over a 2-star sandbagged V9 every single day. Don't get me wrong, I'll climb both, but I'll recommend the V7 over and over while the V9 will be just another tick. Grades have absolutely nothing to do with quality ratings, and for me, quality is a far better reason to climb something.

3. Sanity

Let's be honest here: grades are already confusing enough. Imagine if we tried to consolidate so that all grades are solid. We'd have to create a new grade range for those climbs at the low end of each spectrum. 12b-? V9a+? It's only going to get more complicated with further delineation. I suppose if you really want to, you should just go ahead and do it.

Ultimately, you're free to grade things however you want with whatever system you so desire. Just don't be surprised when nobody wants to discuss why that V6 you just did should only get V5d.

Maybe all of you who are staunch supporters of the stout should just acquiesce to the existence of soft grades. I mean, without them you'd have nothing with which to prop up your teetering egos.

Success or Mastery?

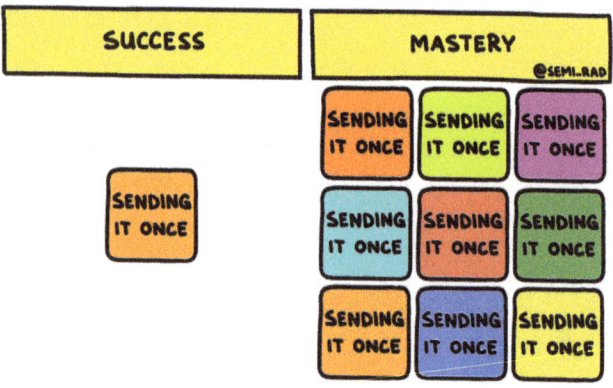

"Oh, I can't get on that – I don't want to unsend it."

I've said it. You've said it.

Climbing is a sport that's built on successes. You do the move, you send the boulder, you win the comp, you look forward.

We rarely take the time to look back.

I often use skateboarding as a metaphor in my workshops and talks because skaters do one important thing much better than climbers.

They chase mastery instead of success.

Unless it's something death defying, a skater doesn't often land a trick and say, "Never doing that again!" They don't worry about unsending that Kickflip or Backside 360. Instead, they do it over and over, in different environments, over new obstacles, and back to back with other tricks.

At some point, the Kickflip was state of the art. Rodney Mullen invented it by accident and called it the Magic Flip because it hardly made sense. He had just learned the flatland Ollie (which he invented as well) and noticed that when he didn't get it quite right the board would flip. By the end of the day he had landed the first Magic Flip. Then he did it 100 times. Then up a curb. Then over an obstacle. Then Kickflip 180. Then 360. Then with two flips. Then Kickflip Underflip. Then two flips and Varial 180. And suddenly (not so suddenly) he could land the basic variations every single time he tried no matter what.

You get the idea. Mastery.

Tony Hawk spent 15 years learning how to do the 900. 15 YEARS between the 720 and 900, which he finally landed in 1999. He could have been happy with that success and walked away from a trick that had broken his bones several times.

Instead, in 2016 at 48 years old, he landed a 900 within one session of deciding to try it again. How? Because he wasn't satisfied with success. He didn't stop at that first 900. He landed more and more, back to back with other tricks, until he had it mastered. Had he been afraid of unsending after landing his first at the X Games in San Francisco, no chance he's doing another 17 years later.

So how can climbers embrace mastery instead of success?

Don't be satisfied with sending the boulder. Send it better. Three or four or more times. Make it damn near perfect. Put it on the circuit. Transform it into a warmup that makes you feel like a superhero.

Revisit old mini projects now and then. Unsend them and then resend them. If you've been on the path of mastery, they'll go faster and you'll be better. Someday that former project might be a warmup.

Mastery. Superhero.

The Send is a Necessary Piece of the Process

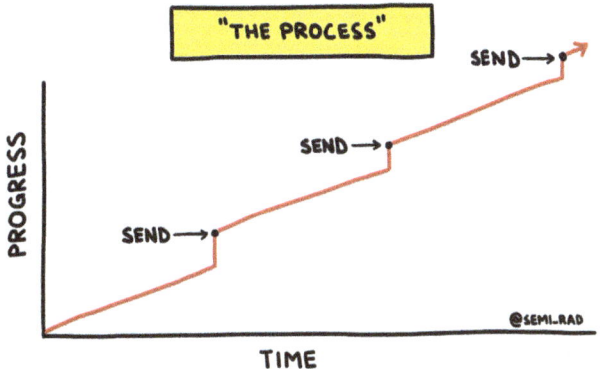

"It's all about the journey."

After carefully curating my Instagram feed to get rid of most of the Moonboarding videos, I've been left with hundreds of posts every day that are trying to sell me the same message.

> *"It's the process that's important."*
> *"It's not about success and failure, it's only about days out with friends."*
> *"Sending doesn't matter because I do it all for the journey."*

Their journey is missing a valuable piece.

The send.

We talk a lot around here about how important it is to place value on the process – on the podcast, with our clients, and during our workshops with other coaches, climbers, and parents. We believe that. Hell, we sell a journal we call the Process Journal. But we also want to send. Denying that is making an excuse for never actually putting yourself on the line.

Why is it that we try to assign value to the goal setting, the training, the work put in to learn the moves and subtleties of each sequence, the scheduling to get to the project, the communication with our partners, battling the jitters we get while tying in – but when we fail, we try to pretend it doesn't matter?

Be honest with yourself. Of course it fucking matters.

We're all trying to improve. Success on a climb is part of that improvement. It's a marker on your journey. If you miss all the markers, you're on the wrong path.

But how do we do this? How can we reconcile caring about the outcome with focusing on the process? My friend Trevor Ragan from *Learner Lab* says that we have to take outcomes seriously – not personally. In our conversation on the podcast, Trevor discusses how scientists view the always moving target of improvement. "They know the outcome is a reflection of the process – not of them as a person," he says. If we look at our sends or failures in the way that a scientist might, it becomes much easier to understand.

If We Fail: Something went wrong in the process. Be clear here – not every process is a good one. Let's make some changes and try to find what is going wrong.

If We Send: Something about the process went right. Let's retest with another goal, try to pin down what we're doing well, and refine it.

Arno Ilgner, author of *The Rock Warrior's Way*, in a conversation on my podcast, defined process-based motivation as "learning based. What do I need to LEARN so that I can achieve that end goal?" Arno obviously cares about the outcome, but he also doesn't take the outcome personally. He sees it as a test of sorts. If we don't "pass the test," it's because something in the process is holding us back.

We're humans. Failure hurts. Pretending it doesn't is a lie. We understand that we need those failures in order to continue learning. It's the same with success. We need those sends not only to keep us afloat, but also to learn what it is that we're doing right.

If you're one of those people on my Instagram feed who never seems to send anything, ask yourself why that is. Something in your process – your journey – is going wrong. Maybe your goals are set too high for now and you need a smaller, intermediate checkpoint. Maybe you're skipping over the important small lessons along the way and jumping straight to failure at the big goal. Take a closer look at the missing piece of your journey.

The same goes for those climbers who send everything they try. Are you pushing hard enough? Are you ever really putting yourself on the line? There is much to be learned from failure, so you may be depriving yourself of valuable lessons.

Just be sure and see it through. Send.

No Kings, No Way

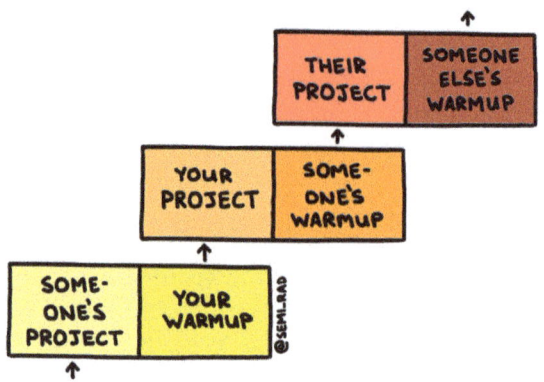

"Comparison is the thief of joy."
— *Theodore Roosevelt*

Around here, we like to use the hashtag *#webuildmachines*. However, I'm acutely aware that you could just as often substitute it with the hashtag *#webuildmonsters*, and I don't mean that in a positive way. Any time that you are working to build up bodies and spirits, and to help people break into new personal levels, it's inevitable that some egos will over-inflate. They'll grow bigger and bigger, heavier and more cumbersome, and eventually, those Hindenburgian egos will come crashing down.

And it's going to hurt.

Let me start by saying this: I've never had a bad day rock climbing, and I've never had a bad day training. Have I performed poorly? Absolutely. Have I sucked at climbing sometimes? Definitely. But I'm in the woods climbing rocks, or I'm at the gym working to better myself. I CHOSE those things. What could possibly make me upset to be there?

You failed on your project, lowered off, dejected, and then somebody warmed up on it. You suck, you'll never be good, you may as well quit.

Don't be an idiot.

That person was once where you are. That wasn't always their warmup, and their project is someone else's warmup.
Don't compare your beginning to someone else's middle.
While I was projecting Transworld Depravity, the hardest route I've sent, I had the pleasure of watching a (then unknown)
Alex Megos flash it as a warmup. I watched several friends send it much faster than I did. This didn't diminish at all the feeling I felt when I finally clipped the chains.

There's another thing it didn't do. It didn't diminish the psyche I felt at seeing a random person send their first 11b, which, incidentally, was my warmup that day. They were inspired to see me climb and downclimb it without chalking, same as I was to watch a young rosy-cheeked Megos walk Transworld Depravity a year prior.

For the last couple of years I've listened over and over to the album *No Kings*, by one of my favorite hip-hop collective, Doomtree. Its concept is simple, one we could all do well to live by:

There are no kings. There are no peasants.

Your battle on your project is no different than Sharma battling on First Round First Minute, or Nalle on his multi-year Lappnor Project, which became Burden of Dreams. It's no different than a beginner slapping and clawing their way up their first 5.9.

This is a personal struggle. If, for some reason, you believe that yours ranks higher than that of someone else then your biggest struggle isn't on the rock at all.

I've built machines. I've also built monsters. Frankly, I feel bad about it. Climbing can't be much fun when you're mostly concerned about how you compare to everyone else.

Selective Learning | The Short-Sighted Approach

Through many conversations about training with friends and other climbers, I've discovered one common thread – you can almost always find a reason to continue training the short-sighted way that you have been.

What I mean is that if you get attached to your method of training, the method that has worked for years and gotten you to where you are (and where you've been for five seasons), then you're probably missing out on some great advice. That is, of course, unless your method is to constantly look for new methods and target new weak areas in your climbing. If that's you, you can just skip this piece. If you're the one who has done exactly the same workout for years and have been stuck at the same grades for most of that time, then you may want to read on.

Just be advised that you might not read exactly what you hope.

I understand the draw to this style of "learning." You pick up a training book, you flip through until you find a passage or a chapter that echoes what you've based all your training on, and you latch onto it.

"That's me! I KNEW I was doing this the right way!"

It's true, you are doing THAT the right way. Thing is – there are hundreds of other facets to your training that you're not paying attention to at all. Not to mention they are all listed right there in that book – you're just looking past them.

You see someone stronger than you, maybe even a pro, doing exactly what you've been doing.

"YES! Sean McColl trains this way, so it MUST be right!"

Absolutely it's right, for him, in that specific moment. I'm betting Sean trains more than just the one thing you've latched onto. You can look at his climbing and see that it's far more complex than just a circuit on an adjustable wall, but you choose to look past that. It must be that one thing that's elevated him to those heights. Of course it is.

Here's what I urge you to do: reread your training books, including this one when you finish it. Reread the training blogs that you frequent. Relisten to our podcast. Completely ignore all the things you already know and take a deeper look at the things that make you uncomfortable. The things you say you don't need. The things you say won't help you. Look past your fears, your hang-ups, and your preconceived notions. Chances are, you know what you're missing. You know because you've argued with yourself about it, and you always win. Let the other you win this time, or at least give her a chance. She might just surprise you.

Climb Better Faster | The Often-Missing Piece

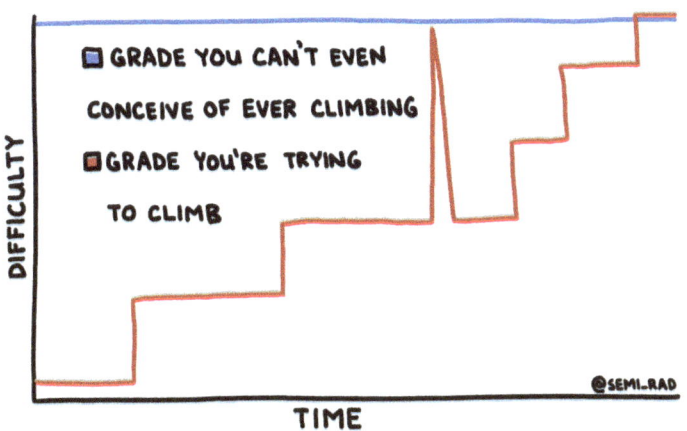

Years ago, I wrote two back to back essays about how to get better faster – *The Magic Bullet* and *Training Wheels*. I thought that I was a genius for pointing out a problem and then offering solutions.

I wasn't.

I failed to take into account that people would actually follow my advice and move on past the level detailed in those essays. I failed to realize that people would ask "Ok, now what?"

You were once a newb, asking for advice in the gym, and you actually followed it. You got better. Fast. You mastered the level you were struggling on. Seven years later (sorry it took so long – I've been busy) I'm here to tell you what's next. It's actually pretty simple.

Try something hard.

Pick a project that inspires you. Something a little over your head that might be intimidating. A grade you wouldn't have dared call realistic when you were taking off the training wheels. Potentially even a grade up from that.

Just try it.

It's going to feel a little ridiculous at first. Maybe even impossible. Try it again. A few more times for good measure.

Now step it down slightly to the grade below and try that. Put some time and effort into it. If progress stalls, reevaluate your tactics. More effort. More time. Mastery. See it through. Outcomes matter.

It's entirely true that if you don't try something hard, you can't do anything hard. A non-negotiable step to climbing V10 or 5.14 is to try V10 or 5.14. It's also true that it's incredibly difficult to prepare for something that you have absolutely no clue about. Now you know. You know what the next level feels like and you've got a good idea of what it will require of you.

But as the great hip-hop philosopher Aesop Rock rhymed:

"Knowing ain't half the battle, that's a bullshit quip written by some asshole."

You have to go try the thing. You have to actually go to battle.

Remember to continue to be honest with yourself. Be kind to yourself. And try really fucking hard.

Goals Not Met | Freedom and Transworld Depravity

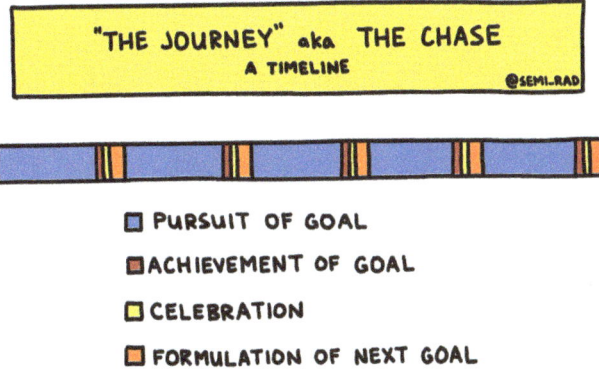

I was through the middle crux for the first time from the ground. The hardest moves were behind me, with only a V5-ish mantle and a 12+-ish headwall guarding the chains. And it was wet. Not damp wet. Soaked wet. Dripping wet.

I'm still not sure how it got that way. It was dry the day before, and I'd decided to hedge my bets on the better temps and better sleep that I could get. It hadn't rained. But there it was, dripping from the mantle onto my face, mocking me.

50 feet prior, at the big rest before the business, I'd had a conversation with a new friend on a neighboring route. She had read my *Don't Squash the Banana* essay and it resonated with her. I hung out there talking to Katy Dannenberg, shaking out, laughing, and generally relaxing, all the while discussing commitment. And then I was climbing, her reassuring voice just beside me as I stuck the move for the first time.

Drip. Drip.

I was this far, my first real chance at sending, and I had to commit. The entire Motherlode had congregated in the cave, anticipating the battle. The wet V5 above me had gotten into my nerves, and I desperately needed a plan. My next shake, on a hold I called The Basketball, had water streaming from it. The Terrible Tooth hold above it was smack dab in the middle of the waterfall. However, I could see that the line of holds out right was dry. If I could just get out there, I could recover on the first two good edges before launching into the final terrible crimps.

The mantle never felt easier. I didn't hesitate, just executed. Instead of my normal kneescum-handjam-layback rest on The Basketball, I kept moving, barely making the hard, lateral reach off of The Tooth to the in-cut edges I intended to rest on.

Both in-cuts were filled with tiny, taunting puddles.

I tried to recover but my mind was spinning. 12 feet from victory, past the wet rock, and I was going to fail. Many of my best friends were watching. My fiancé was on belay. I had battled my heart out to get to this spot. Knowing I would have no opportunity to dry my fingers before taking the worst of the grips, I committed once more. I crimped hard, pasted my foot on the good smear, lunged, and I fell.

The moans of the gathered crowd echoed throughout the cave. "Do over!" someone shouted. "You were robbed," Dan Mirsky told me, "but at least now you know it's possible."

And then the weather turned toward summer, without so much as a glance over its shoulder at me.

For weeks it was a mind fuck. I was two moves from a long-time goal, and I had the experience of reaching it – I just didn't quite close the deal. Did I want to get back on it? Was there any reason to finish it? Was it really the experience and the progression I was after, or does the number itself mean something to me?

For nearly a month, I wasn't sure I'd go back. However, while standing in the shower after a gym session, I came to a realization. I really loved climbing on that route. Sending it was essentially a formality, and I'd already had the send experience, but I WANTED to go back and climb on it.

It had long been a goal to climb 5.14 by the age of 40. As my 40th birthday came and went, several people asked me if I was bummed not to make good on my goal.

Goals aren't made to be met. When I meet a goal, I celebrate by moving the bar higher. It's become incredibly cliché to say that it's all about the journey, and I'm not so sure I completely agree. It isn't only about the journey. For me, it's about a chase. It's about being eluded. It's about some chunk of rock showing me who's boss until it decides to allow my passage. It's about reaching past my own perceived limits and realizing that I can change my own perceptions. So no, I'm not bummed at all. Quite the opposite.

21 days after my random deadline passed, I climbed 5.14. After eight years of sport climbing, with 65 5.13's under my belt, Transworld Depravity, a Bill Ramsey masterpiece in the Red River Gorge's Madness Cave, decided that I'd grown up enough, and it allowed me to climb from bottom to top without falling off.

In the end, I never had to fight. While I'm usually vocal, this time, other than deliberate breathing, I didn't make a sound. As is often reported, it felt eerily easy. Like I could do it again, and maybe I will. Maybe not. There are cracks to be climbed. Hard boulders to do. Music to be made, and books to be written. A new life to build. Other climbers, still reaching for their ultimate goals, to help prepare. So many worthy opponents.

First, I'll set a few more ridiculous goals.

Afterword

Originally, the subtitle of this book was *Easy Ways to Become a Better Climber*. My friend Tyler pointed out that while he often finds my advice simple, he rarely finds it easy. We immediately changed the subtitle. To be perfectly honest, I often look back on these essays and feel as if maybe I'm being too repetitive or too harsh. Then I remember how often – thousands of times over the past few years – that I've had to reiterate these ideas to my friends, clients, and to myself. Yes, these are simple concepts. Not easy. In most cases, it's these ideas that usher in the biggest changes.

Change. Another simple but not easy concept. Like I mentioned in the introduction, I believe in it. Fiercely. But it's not going to happen unless you want it. Unless you want to fight for it. To see the entire process through. To care about the outcome.

I'm on this journey with you. I'm a work in progress. Constant re-evaluation. Head down but eyes up, driving forward with knowledge of what's in the rear-view, taking care to be the best I can and not expecting more.

Acknowledgements

I've got too many ideas and not enough time, but there are a handful of people who hold me accountable to some of these ideas in different ways. Without them, this book, this company, this systematic dream chasing couldn't happen.

My wife, Annalissa, who somehow puts up with my insatiable need to be creating something, tells me that she's proud of what I've built just enough to keep me going – but not so much that I can rest on my laurels.

My daughter, Katy, who I work hard to be an example for. She told me that sometimes I need to "soften the blow," but for some reason still comes to me for doses of reality. I try to soften them. Sometimes.

The whole team at Power Company Climbing. I never envisioned it as a team in the beginning, but I'm damned sure happy that it is. Sometimes it seems a little out of control, but if it didn't, we'd all be bored silly.

Brendan Leonard, whom I bonded with over a love of hip-hop, and whose illustrations brought much needed color to these essays. For 20 years I made my living as an artist while Brendan made his as a writer. He somehow agreed to trade places with me for this project. That he finds my perspectives worthy is an honor.

And most of all, the community of people who've supported this thing I've been building. I've written essays, recorded podcasts, made videos, and created products because of you. It's because you cared to hear what I had to say that I took care in saying it. That I'll continue to say it, make it, do it, build it. This book is the first. Certainly not the last.

Thanks for keeping me accountable.

About the Author

A climber of nearly 25 years, Kris Hampton fancies himself a modern-day renaissance man, having love affairs with painting, music, writing, and now building a business. He discovered his interest in movement via skateboarding and gymnastics, and now through Power Company Climbing helps thousands of climbers find their potential, which is as great a source of joy for him as sending his own projects. Addicted to learning via recording face to face conversations for the Power Company Podcast, he's climbed 5.14 and V-double-digits and is currently trying to avoid the old-folks endurance retirement home by focusing on climbing harder boulders in his mid-40's. This is his first book, but he has no plans to make it his last.

About the Artist

Brendan Leonard is an award-winning storyteller, author and filmmaker, and a must-stop on your daily Instagram scroll (assuming you're able to laugh at yourself). As the creator of *Semi-Rad.com*, he's (accurately) been referred to as the voice of our generation of outdoor adventurers. A former contributing editor for *Climbing Magazine*, he's also written about climbing for *Alpinist*, *Outside*, *National Geographic Adventure*, and *CNN.com*. His books range from the trademark pointed humor of *Bears Don't Care About Your Problems* to the introspective inspiration of *Sixty Meters to Anywhere*. Addicted to collecting vintage hip-hop vinyl, he has a love/hate relationship with running long distances and is currently working on making things.

www.ingramcontent.com/pod-product-compliance
Lightning Source LLC
Chambersburg PA
CBHW061233070526
44584CB00030B/4109